FROM MOTHER TO DAUGHTER

Also by Katie Piper

Beautiful
Things Get Better
Start Your Day with Katie
Beautiful Ever After
Confidence

FROM MOTHER TO DAUGHTER

The things I'd tell my child

Katie Piper

With Diane Piper

Quercus

First published in Great Britain in 2018 by

Quercus Editions Ltd
Carmelite House
50 Victoria Embankment
London EC4Y 0DZ

An Hachette UK company

A CIP catalogue record for this book is available
from the British Library

HB ISBN 978 1 78747 061 3
TPB ISBN 978 1 78429 656 8

10 9 8 7 6 5 4 3 2 1

Editorial Consultant: Caro Handley
Psychological Consultant: Dr Kairen Cullen

Text designed and typeset by CC Book Production

Printed and bound in the UK by Clays Ltd, St Ives plc

I would like to dedicate this book to my own mother and my two daughters. Mum, thank you for always being there for me, for teaching me, loving me and letting me fly.

All that I am is because of you.

Belle and Penelope, you came into my life and enriched it in a way only a mother can understand. I love you both with all my heart.

Contents

Introduction

Becoming a mother has been the most amazing journey for me.

From the moment I knew my first baby was a girl I started to plan, and to hope and dream. I wanted so much for her – health, friendships, love, work she enjoys – in other words a meaningful and fulfilling life. And, of course, it was just the same the second time around, all those dreams still firmly in place, despite the extra circles under my eyes from lack of sleep, the battered toes from falling over stray toys and the soundtrack from *Frozen* stuck on a loop in my head.

Near the top of my list of hopes and dreams for my girls, Belle and Penelope, is the wish for us to enjoy the same great relationship I had with my mum, Diane. The mother–daughter bond is something special, and I couldn't wait to experience it with my own daughters. But I also knew that the world had changed so much since I was growing up. What would I need to know, to learn, to understand in order to give my daughters the strength to cope with everything that might come their way?

I want my daughters to be strong, brave women who can speak up for themselves and navigate life's ups and downs with confidence. The world can be a tough place, and something unexpected can come along and change everything, so I want them to be able to take life in their stride, the good and the bad, and still keep their centre of gravity – the calm place inside that knows 'I am me, whatever happens'.

Of course, like almost every parent, I feel protective. I don't want anyone to hurt my daughters, ever. But the truth is they will get hurt. I can't protect them from a mean comment, a job that doesn't work out, a failed relationship. All I can do is teach them how to deal with those things when they happen. The way you manage adversity is the best measure of anyone, because if you can come through the toughest of times in one piece, you can cope with anything.

I know that the example I set my girls, in all things, will be vital. But what do I teach them about friendships, relationships and a woman's role? And how do I help them navigate a world that is changing so fast?

Before writing this book I did a lot of exploring, talking and looking around. I talked to friends, to experts and to mothers – young and older. And I've included some of their stories in the book, because there's nothing like someone else's insight to help you see what's happening in your own life. Many of us are single parents, caring for children alone and that's a tough call. There are times when I find it hard even with the support of a loving, involved partner, so I have enormous respect for the mums, and the dads, who do it alone.

Some of the most valuable insight and advice came from psychologist Kairen Cullen, who has vast experience of working with mothers and daughters of all ages. Her quiet wisdom and spot-on observations have been a huge help.

I also talked to my mum, Diane. Who better to turn to for mother–daughter advice? We talked about our own relationship and Mum's relationship with her own mother. It's fascinating to follow a line of women, from my grandmother, to my mother, to me, and then my daughters. Each one of those relationships is different to the others, and yet they are all built around the unique mother–daughter dynamic. Loving together, sharing, talking, laughing – infuriating each other at times – but such an important relationship for both of us, and at the heart of the way we see ourselves and the world.

I talked to Mum about how she did things when she was a young mother, and how she feels now, looking back on bringing up me, my brother and my sister? She's been amazing, always there for me through everything, steadily by my side. I hope I can do that for my own two girls.

I've asked Mum to contribute her thoughts to the book, adding her own special angle on subjects that are close to her heart. We've added a chapter on coping with trauma, as many of us find ourselves having to do, and Mum will have a lot to say there. We've included extracts from the diary she kept after my acid attack, which I hope will help others going through unexpected tragedy. She'll also share what it was like when I left home twice – the first time as an excited teenager, the second time putting a foot tentatively back out in the world, two years after the attack. I think Mum felt a lot of concern then, about how tough life might be for me as I rebuilt my life.

Mum is also a doting grandmother to Belle and Penelope and she has given me so much good advice – I couldn't have done it without her. But they're still very young and I'm still in the early stages of the motherhood journey, whereas Mum is a few steps ahead of me and can talk about what it's like having adult daughters.

I think Mum would agree that bringing up happy, healthy daughters has become more challenging. Girls today have more opportunities than those in any previous generation. But they also face unprecedented pressures. They're expected to become top executives, surgeons and judges, and at the same time to be slim and attractive and to know how to navigate the world of online communications.

That's why I want to look at what it means to raise a daughter in the modern world, what we learn as mothers and the incredible power of mother–daughter relationships.

I've looked at many of the issues we mums face in raising our daughters; issues such as body image, the pressures of social media, role models, dating, sex and safety, and mental health. I've also looked at the power of the internet (and how to use it wisely), the work/parenting balance and how to teach girls to speak out and to be part of the big conversations in life about the things that matter.

Although my focus is on daughters in this book, I should mention that much of the information, insight and advice I've discovered and brought together is equally true for sons. Boys also face a tough world and many challenges as they grow, and parents have just as many concerns for their sons as they do for their daughters.

We all know there's no such thing as the perfect mother–daughter relationship; each one is unique and that's what makes them special. Some mums and daughters have such an intense relationship that they seem to live in one another's pockets. Others have so much space that they can go for weeks or months without seeing one another. But the bond is there, no matter what, and none of us would be without it.

CHAPTER

Becoming a Mum

The moment my daughter Belle was put into my arms I realized that everything in my world had changed. Life had suddenly stopped being about me, it was all about this tiny, perfect person staring up at me with such trust.

So many mixed emotions swirled through my head. I felt so grateful to have a child – I had known for so long that I might never become a mum that it was almost impossible to believe it had actually happened, and yet here she was, my beautiful baby. I wanted to give her everything – to show her the world, to protect her, to help her grow into a strong, brave woman. And at the same time, I felt helpless. I didn't even know how to feed her or change her nappy and the thought of taking her home was terrifying. How was I going to take responsibility for this amazing small person when I felt so unprepared and overwhelmed by what lay ahead?

It was the start of a lifelong journey, and I could only begin one step at a time. I looked at Richie, smiling down at the two of us, and I knew that we'd get there together – getting to know our daughter, learning to care for her and bringing her up to be a happy, healthy woman who can find her own path in life.

I had already bonded closely with her while I was expecting. I talked to her all the time, peered at the scans, trying to make out her features, delighted in every kick I felt her give and was amazed by my growing bump. But none of that prepared me for the reality of meeting her for the first time – her soft, downy skin, little tufts of hair, huge, curious eyes. She seemed to me like an absolute angel and I hoped that she and I would always be close and share a special bond.

For most women becoming a mum is just as special as it was for me. A unique experience and completely life-changing. And that's true, however you become a mum. I have friends who have adopted children – I thought at one point that I would take that route too – and other friends who have become mothers with the help of a surrogate, and in each case the experience is just as powerful and emotional as it was for me. A child coming into your life, by whatever means, is a miracle.

For me it felt especially lovely to have a daughter. A girl to share girly things with, to gossip and chat with as she grew older. A girl to dress in gorgeous clothes and to giggle with. A girl to bring up in a world where her choices are bigger and brighter than ever before. A girl who can be whatever she wants to be in life.

The Mother–Daughter Bond

There's something very special about the bond between mother and daughter. Most of us who have it take it for granted, but that doesn't make it any less special. It's a bond of shared womanhood, shared experiences and emotions, and shared understanding. It can be deeply satisfying and at the same time deeply frustrating.

Throughout history, the mother–daughter bond has been seen as special and it's a relationship often portrayed in films – look at Donna and Sophie in *Mamma Mia!*, Tess and Anna in *Freaky Friday* (switching roles – something we could probably all do with), Daphne and Milly in *Because I Said So*, Adele and Ann in *Anywhere But Here*, Aurora and Emma in *Terms of Endearment*, Elinor and Merida in *Brave* (this is a good one to watch with a little girl) – I could go on and on. Then there's television; remember *Absolutely Fabulous*, with crazy Edina and her super-sensible daughter Saffy? And as for the celebrity mums and their daughters, they seem to be everywhere – Jerry Hall with her model offspring Elizabeth and Georgia, Kate Moss and Lila Grace, Reese Witherspoon and Ava. All posing beautifully and almost certainly all destined to share the joys and exasperations of the unique mother–daughter bond.

It's from our mothers that we learn what it is to be a woman. And the relationship can be so powerful that it influences everything in our lives: our self-esteem, health and life choices. And, of course, it also influences many of our other relationships. The way we behave in adult relationships, the way we mother our

3

own children and the way we see ourselves are all profoundly influenced by our mothers.

This has now been proven by science. New research shows that mothers and daughters share a structure of the brain that regulates emotions. A study published in the *Journal of Neuroscience* in 2016 found that the association between mothers and daughters was significantly greater than that between mothers and sons, fathers and daughters or fathers and sons. This means that women are more likely to understand and relate to the emotions of their mothers, or daughters, than anyone else. And it creates a powerful bond, for better or worse.

The love between a mother and her daughter is special. But that doesn't mean it's always easy – far from it. The relationship can be emotionally intense and full of unrealistic expectations. We sometimes want our mothers, and our daughters, to be perfect, and that's never possible.

At five a daughter adores her mother, at fifteen she may well feel that her mother is always doing embarrassing things, or doesn't understand her. Mothers and daughters can, and do, fall out spectacularly and it sometimes takes years for the relationship to settle into something comfortable once the daughter is an adult. The mother–daughter relationship can be the source of the greatest love and the deepest anger we feel in our lives.

The mother–daughter dynamic has been around for as long as time. But in the end every mother–daughter relationship is unique and just that bit different to any other.

I was incredibly lucky with my mum. She was warm, generous and loving when I was little and she patiently put up with my teenage strops and demands, always there, along with my dad, like a backbone in my life.

Sometimes the world in which a mother brings up a daughter can be very different to the world in which she herself grew up. My mum was raised by rather formal parents who, typically for the time, did not spend a lot of time with her. I think it made her determined to be there for her own children, so when we came along – first my brother, then me, then my sister – she created a warm, safe and close world for us in which our parents were always there.

So what did I want for Belle? I pictured the two of us in a warm, loving relationship for life, always there for one another, under-standing and supporting one another. Mother and daughter and best friends too. A little candy-coloured dream bubble. But I had to remind myself that in real life it doesn't go that way. Mothers and daughters have ups and downs and that's all normal. What matters is that underneath it all, they love one another to bits. So in the end what I realized I truly wanted was for us to be able to talk to one another, always, and for her to feel absolutely sure of my love, and to know that I would always be there for her.

Becoming a Mother

When Richie and I got together we both wanted children. We'd both come from close, loving families and we wanted to pass that on to our own children. But after all I had been through in the previous few years – the trauma, injury, skin grafts, multiple operations and anti-rejection drugs – I had been told that I might not be able to conceive. I knew I had to accept that, but I wanted to be a mum so much, I was determined it would happen one way or another.

For a long time I had thought I wouldn't even get married, let alone come as far as trying for a baby. After my acid attack, in 2008, I almost died, and my recovery was long and painful. When I was finally able to make decisions about life again I had lost everything – my home, work, social life, the lot. Friends had moved on and were marrying and having children and I was just taking baby steps back to finding some kind of independence. And the first couple of dates I went on were a disaster. It took all my courage to try again, but then I met Richie – kind, funny and warm, and we just clicked. We got together, then moved in together, and starting a family seemed the obvious next step.

In the end the pregnancy happened soon after we decided to try for a baby. When I began to suspect that I might be pregnant I hardly dared to believe it. I rushed out and bought three pregnancy tests and then locked myself in the bathroom with them. When they were all positive I told Richie. The two of us were stunned; excited and happy, but at the same time both thinking, 'Help, we've got to do this now. There's no going back.'

I shot straight off to the doctor where I had another test. 'Yes, you're pregnant,' they said. 'What next?' I asked, all excited. 'Nothing next,' they said. 'You're only six weeks along, come back in another few months.' I was a bit startled, until I realized that to them I was just another pregnant woman and that felt great, because it was all so normal. My experience of medical things had been very grim and for a long time I hadn't had the luxury of normal. I practically skipped home, I was so happy.

The nine months of pregnancy were quite a journey for me. From that moment on I was on alert. I was scared that something might go wrong, so I was careful about everything I did. In restaurants I would be on my phone to check what I could eat and what I should avoid. The foods pregnant women should not eat tend to change with time, so I was constantly looking for the latest updates (unpasteurized cheese, raw eggs, pâté, liver . . .) and trying to do everything perfectly. And it wasn't just food. I didn't know what exercise was OK and whether I could walk on the treadmill (yes), or go running (yes), or if there was anything I should avoid (heavy weights, any exercise lying on your back after the first three months).

I had lots of blood tests and check-ups and took every recommendation very seriously.

Richie was just the same. He cooked for me and had to keep checking that all the ingredients were alright. We were a couple of novices finding our way through the maze of first pregnancy, determined to get everything right and being ridiculously cautious.

The second time around, when I was pregnant with Penelope, I was so much more relaxed. I still ate healthily and looked after myself (although in the early months the only thing that stopped me feeling sick was eating cartloads of pastries) but I didn't check every five minutes and I forgot all about the blood test results.

Both pregnancies were very normal. With Belle I was filming the series *Bodyshockers* and my face went all red and rashy – the hormone changes – which was a bit tricky, but it passed and apart from that everything was fine.

Pregnancy did make me feel exhausted at times, and a bit moody too. There really are a lot of hormone surges and changes going on in your body, so being moody is part of the whole package, a bit like suddenly craving a food you used to loathe. You're driven by emotion during pregnancy and I got pretty irritable every now and then, which I'm sure meant I wasn't much fun to live with. Richie had to be very patient.

The second time around I was even more tired. Not surprising since Belle was three and absolutely full of energy. I wanted to do everything with her just as usual, but sometimes I just had to hand her over to Richie or Mum and sneak off for a snooze. We told Belle about it fairly early on. We wanted her to be a part of it all, and if anything had gone wrong we would have explained that to her too. As it was, once she got over the excitement there was a new baby in Mummy's tummy, she lost interest until my bump got bigger. Then she would kiss and hug the baby and say she was going to be the best ever big sister. Thankfully she didn't get jealous; she saved that for the cute little dog we got not long before we knew about my second pregnancy.

Then there's the nesting – collecting baby clothes, nappies, toys and the crazy amount of stuff you decide you need for one small child. I loved all that and couldn't resist buying every adorable little outfit I saw.

Like other expectant mums, I went along to all my antenatal appointments and scans and as the due date approached I got more and more excited. But the most valuable 'antenatal' advice I had was from psychologist Kairen Cullen, who reminded me of some of the most important things about becoming a mum.

Before Your Baby Arrives

Preparing for motherhood is unique. It can't be compared with training for a sporting event, an examination or an interview. It means adapting to a whole life change and having confidence and faith in a positive outcome, as well as support from friends and family.

Here are some useful questions to ask yourself when you are preparing to become a mum:

- How will you use to the full your unique self: your experiences, your learning and your beliefs and values?
- How will you prepare yourself physically, emotionally, financially and practically for motherhood?
- How do you decide which aspects of your mother's mothering you wish to repeat and which to adapt or even change?
- What kind of support do you need? Social/emotional/practical/financial?
- How will you keep perspective and be realistic, accepting that you are a good enough mother and not perfect?

Some of these were easy for me – others I had to think long and hard about. I'm a bit of a perfectionist, so accepting that this role I was about to begin – being a mum – was full of potential pitfalls and heartache and failure, as well as all the good stuff, wasn't easy. But it helped me to be more realistic. I didn't want to expect perfection, only to then come crashing down. So I worked hard on 'good enough' as the way forward. And that's been incredibly valuable ever since.

EXERCISE:
A CARING CIRCLE

This exercise is a useful way to think about who is in your life and that of your new baby. After doing the exercise you can think about what it reveals – are there too many people, too few, not enough who are truly close? Is there someone you might bring closer?

A strong circle of caring people around you will give you the support and love a new mother needs.

Take a large piece of plain paper and a marker pen. Draw a circle in the centre and then represent – either with drawing or text – yourself, the baby and the baby's other parent. Choose different coloured markers and draw circles for others involved in yours and your family's lives. Place these circles nearer or further away in relation to your own circle, to represent how important/involved they are. You can extend the activity by making a list of what these different people contribute to you and your family's wellbeing. You might extend this exercise by finding a way of acknowledging and thanking everyone involved.

A-N-T-E-N-A-T-A-L

This mnemomic is a great way of remembering all the things that matter most when you are becoming a mum:

Affirmation – 'I will be a great mum and perfect for my child'

Nutrition of the highest quality

Tenderness to and from yourself and significant others, e.g. other parent, mother, extended family

Empathy – this is a time when having one's needs understood and anticipated is particularly precious and welcomed

Nature – if possible, try to spend some time every day in nature in order to gain perspective, tranquility and peace of mind

Alone time is important – meditation and mindfulness can be helpful

Together time is also important – choose wisely and spend time with those people who bring you joy and calm

Advice from trusted sources – professional and personal that is right for you at the time you need it

Love – yourself, your family and friends and this special time

Being a mother is a dynamic, ever-changing process with different demands, challenges and rewards at every stage. The pregnancy is just the start, but it's as important as every other stage. So look after yourself, nourish yourself, bond with your baby and get some sleep while you can!

The Birth

When Belle was born, I had a planned caesarean – my doctors thought it the safest option given my medical history – and I was expecting a terrible time. I'd read all kinds of horror stories – all about how they cut through the muscle wall and you have a great big scar and you can't lift or bend – and I was very worried. But in the end, it was fine. I'd had so many operations – some of them tough and complicated and incredibly painful – so this one felt like a piece of cake in comparison (and the scar was small!). I was also up and about very soon afterwards, so I was delighted.

After the operation, Richie cut the cord and then they handed her to me. There was a blue sheet up, so I heard her before I saw her; no question, she had healthy lungs. And when I did see her I just melted – she was so small and so adorable. But after a bit I wanted someone to take her back because I didn't know what to do next! The idea that I was going to take her home and do *everything* for her seemed impossible.

A little while later, after she'd been cleaned up a bit, they brought her to me to feed. Another hurdle, but it went fine; she latched on and then proceeded to gorge herself for the next few days.

I was besotted from the start, and I don't doubt it would have been just the same if my baby had been a boy. But I did feel a lovely sense of connection with Belle, and later again with Penelope, because they were my daughters. I knew I was going to love every minute of being their mum, and I hoped I would be worthy of them and do a good job.

After a night in hospital I wanted to go home. I knew I'd recover quicker in my own home. But that also meant Richie and I would be looking after Belle on our own. It was like being given a job you have never even tried, and you're expected to know how to do it.

I kept thinking, why are they trusting us? Is anyone going to check that we're doing it right?

Of course, there are all kinds of checks (health visitors) and sources of help (family, friends, the internet), but basically this is it, you and your baby, getting on with the rest of your life together.

The First Three Months

The first few days at home were a blur of feeding, tiredness, family – mine and Richie's – coming and going. Then suddenly – at least it seemed sudden to me – everyone was gone and Richie's two weeks off were over and I was on my own with Belle. The days stretched out and, feeling a bit alone and not quite sure what to do, I decided I should keep her interested and entertained. So I put on DVDs, played with building blocks and showed her picture books, reading the stories to her, even though she had no idea what I was on about.

With hindsight I realize she'd have been just as happy if I'd played Michael Jackson instead of 'Old Macdonald', and watched a film I wanted to catch up on instead of *Postman Pat*. But I took it all *sooo* seriously. And I didn't realize then that I should have grabbed my chances in those early days, because once Belle was old enough to choose for herself we ended up listening to endless re-runs of Disney CDs, in the car, in the house – I knew them all word for word.

The next time around, with Penelope, I was a lot more relaxed! The joy of the second one is that you know so much more about the whole process and don't feel nearly as anxious about getting it all perfect.

I took hundreds of photos of Belle. I used to walk every day to the local photo shop; I must have been their most frequent customer. Every inch of wall space in our house was filled with pictures; I never tired of looking at her. Then once I had Penelope I realized I had to even things up and take just as many!

I took maternity leave so that I would have a few months just getting to know Belle (and again later with Penelope). At first, I found the early mornings – and I mean 5am most days – tough after being able to sleep until a civilized time. But in time Richie and I both adjusted. He was great about doing his share; when I got up to feed the girls in the night he'd get up too, get me a glass of water and sit with me. I think at the beginning he was worried I'd fall asleep on the baby! But once I got used to expressing milk, he would do some of the night feeds himself. Mum always told me Dad was very hands on too, and I was glad I'd married a man who was the same.

We really enjoy parenting the girls together. Parenting isn't a perfect art and you're expected to do it with no training. Most of the time you have to muddle through, doing your best, and if there are two of you it makes the responsibility a little bit less scary. You've got one another's backs, you can step in and say 'you're tired, go and have a rest and I'll take over'.

When Belle was about six weeks old, Mum came to stay for a couple of weeks. She and Dad had come to meet Belle when she was born, but at that time Mum was in the middle of medical treatment, so it wasn't until later that she could come to stay and really get to know Belle. Luckily Mum felt well and she was a fantastic help and a fount of knowledge, having brought up her own three.

The first thing I said to her was, 'I'm sorry – I totally get it now.'

She laughed at that. It's not until you have your own baby that you realize what's involved, and what lies ahead. Mum was always so patient with us, she was always there, she put us first, and when I had Belle I understood what that meant. I wanted to thank her for the stability she and Dad had provided, which made me feel safe and loved.

Once Mum arrived I stopped Googling questions about baby-care and just asked her. And I continued to do that – I called her every time I got stuck or needed to know what to do with the girls – and Mum always had the answer. She never pushed advice onto me, she let me do it my way, but she was on hand to help when I needed it.

Diane says:

It was wonderful seeing Katie with a baby of her own – and I loved becoming a grandmother.

Seeing Belle and then Penelope when they were each born reminded me of when I had had Katie – she appeared to be looking around and the midwife said, 'She's been here before.' She was always interested in everything around her, and she was such a laid-back and placid baby that she even fell asleep when I was changing her nappy.

It has been fascinating to see the changes that have happened in the years since I became a young mum. Katie was born in 1983 and by then I'd already had her brother Paul, who is a couple of years older.

I really enjoyed being pregnant and watching my bump grow and delighted in buying floaty maternity dresses. I loved feeling special; I was nurturing new life and welcomed all the changes that went with it. Katie and her sister Suzy, on the other hand, wore tight figure-hugging clothes when they were pregnant and talked about being fat. They didn't want to know how much they weighed and groaned when something didn't fit any more! I don't think the same pressure was there when I was their age, my friends and I wore loose dresses and laughed about our baby bumps. There was no pressure to lose baby weight, we assumed we'd lose it naturally while we were busy looking after our babies.

By the time I had three I had my hands full, but I loved it. Although I was a teacher, I was never interested in climbing the career ladder. As long as we could pay the bills and feed the kids that was all that mattered. I went to jumble sales and fêtes where I would buy toys, games and dressing-up clothes for the children for a few pence. But with the girls' pregnancies I found myself caught up in the pressures of having a baby in the 21st century, making sure the girls had everything they could possibly need and occasionally wondering, how did I manage without half these things?

It's meant a lot to me to be there for Katie and Suzy, because my own mother was rather old fashioned and so I didn't turn to her for advice. But then I have sometimes wondered whether Katie might have felt that some of my advice was a bit outdated too? If she did feel that, she was very tactful and didn't say so! Of course, now you can have pregnancy apps on your phone which give you all the information you could possibly need. I just had a couple of rather dull books from the library.

I was reminded of how overwhelming it can be with a new baby when Katie phoned me, a few weeks after Belle was born, to say, 'I can't even go to the toilet! I can't leave Belle, she cries when I put her in the chair.' I think she felt that if Belle was crying she had to hold her the whole time. I told her to put Belle down for a bit, she would survive while Katie went to the loo or did whatever she needed to do. I did say to her that it's important to talk to babies. Katie said, 'What do I talk to her about?' I replied, 'Anything! Give her a running commentary on what you are doing or read your emails out loud. She won't mind.'

Advice

It's interesting that Mum relied on her friends, rather than her own mum, for advice. I've been so glad to have her to turn to; she's always been warm and easy to talk to. But, of course, one person can't solve everything, and having a range of friends and family to offer support when you are a new mum is ideal. This is where extended families can be handy – grandparents, uncles, aunts, cousins. And friends of all ages, those who've had children and those who haven't. Everyone has something to offer, so don't be afraid to ask for help when it all gets on top of you – and there are always times when it gets too much. Whether you need a sounding board, a sympathetic ear or someone to go to the shops or hold the baby while you grab a nap, remember that most people like being asked to help out and will do it if they can.

This is especially important for single mums, or those whose partners are not around much. Don't isolate yourself, there are always people around who will lend a hand or just come in for a chat.

There are, of course, times when advice is given, whether you want it or not! Mum was brilliant at holding back until I asked for advice, but I have one or two friends whose mums waded in, keen to take over and explain how every single thing should be done. It wasn't easy for the new mums to tell their own mums to back off. One didn't even try; she just let her mum go ahead and counted the days until she left. But another did talk to her mum, thanking her for everything she'd done and explaining that she could manage and would ask for advice when she needed it. It took a couple of attempts before her mum got the message and stepped back a little.

It's a good idea to spend time with people you trust, who will be a sounding board and offer sympathy without necessarily telling you what to do. Shared problem-solving can simply mean having the chance to talk things over, and the solution will often become clear.

When you are given advice, be selective. You can smile and thank the person without feeling you have to do what they suggest.

CHAPTER 2

Strong, Brave Girls

I want my daughters to grow up to be confident, self-aware and open-minded women, who are loved and loving. I want them to have courage and strength, to have work they enjoy and to be able to contribute generously to their families and to society.

When Belle and Penelope were born, I was full of thoughts and dreams about the way I wanted them to grow up and to see the world. I wanted them to be able to stand up for themselves, to refuse to tolerate injustice and to choose meaningful work that they enjoyed. I wanted them to be independent and self-reliant, but at the same time to have fulfilling relationships. Like every other mother, I wanted their lives to be wonderful. But I also knew that, inevitably, they would have to face disappointment, sadness, hurt and rejection. There will be the job they don't get, the boyfriend who lets them down or the race they don't win. So I want to prepare them for this, I want them to be resilient women who know how to get back up and carry on when life is tough.

Things have changed so much since my mum gave birth to me. Technology, women's rights, and the way we work – all these have transformed our world. And it is still changing. Some things are real positives; women now do jobs that they rarely, if ever, did thirty years ago, let alone when my mum was born in the 1950s. Women today have more ability to direct their own lives and to make choices around the kind of lifestyle they want. It's easier to live openly if you are gay, or to remain single, or to travel the world. On the other hand, thirty years ago we didn't fear terrorism the way we do now, we weren't dealing with internet trolls and we were less stressed and rushed.

I want my daughters to be kind, honest, tolerant and understanding. But what else do I want for them, in a world where all too often what we hear about is intolerance and judgement. How will I teach them to value and appreciate the diversity in the world with open minds and warm hearts?

When I knew I was going to be a mother I thought a lot about the values and beliefs I had inherited and those I wanted to pass on. What did I feel was important in life when I was very young? What kind of beliefs did I have about the way I should be and act in the world? Were there new values or beliefs I added as I became an adult?

The strong identification between mothers and daughters means that I will be the prime influence in the girls' lives. Their dad is vital to their happiness and wellbeing and they're lucky to have a hands-on father who adores them. But they will grow up looking to me as their role model.

A friend of mine, the mother of a ten-year-old daughter, recently split up from a very distant, cold and unemotional man. She went into therapy and told her therapist, 'I don't want my daughter to choose someone like her dad.' The therapist said, 'She will do what you do. So if you want her to choose someone different, someone more emotionally connected and involved, make a different choice yourself, in your next relationship.'

Put that way, it's a big responsibility. Looking at my two small girls, bubbling with life and energy, I want to teach them everything I can about being brave and strong as a woman in today's world.

Values and Beliefs

It's worth taking a moment to talk about what these are because they are at the basis of everything we think and do and all our actions and decisions.

Values and beliefs are often used interchangeably, but they're not quite the same thing, although most of us use both to guide our actions and behaviour and to form our attitudes towards life and the events in our lives.

Beliefs
Beliefs are firmly held opinions, the acceptance that something exists or is true, regardless of whether you have proof. So you might believe in God, or that it's better for a mother to work outside the home (or not) or that couples should stay together no matter what.

21

Beliefs can be positive or negative and can encompass everything from politics to religion to family life.

We tend to hold beliefs that have been passed on by people we trust (parents and other authority figures like teachers or religious leaders) and we often don't question them unless something happens that makes us ask whether our beliefs are right. Children inherit a set of beliefs from their parents or carers and these will influence the way they will feel about themselves. So parents who believe children are precious and should be cared for are more likely to have children who feel good about themselves, and parents who believe it's OK to mistreat children by, for instance, smacking them, shouting at them or ignoring them, will have children with low self-esteem.

Values

Values are principles or standards of behaviour that we all hold. We make a judgement about what is important in life, often based on our beliefs, and this creates our values. For instance, if it is your belief that it's wrong to let other people down, then your values will include dependability.

When you are true to your own values, you will feel good about yourself. But when you aren't, unhappiness sets in. Someone whose values include honesty and transparency is going to feel bad about doing something dishonest; it will eat away at them because there's a mismatch between what they believe and value and what they are doing.

Most of the time we don't think about these things, but taking time to reflect on what your beliefs and values are can be worthwhile, because as a parent you are going to be passing these on.

The Test

Each mother must create her own particular type of mothering to fit her particular situation, her personal history and her own hopes and dreams. Psychologist Kairen Cullen told me, 'I've worked with thousands of mothers and what has struck me is the range and quantity of their unique beliefs about what is important to the job of parenting.'

So, it is worth taking some time to think about what's important to you as a mother, and what your values and beliefs are as far as mothering goes. A very quick way to know whether or not you are mothering in a way that reflects your values is to think about a time when you were happy, proud and fulfilled by your experience as a mother. This time will be one in which your actions matched your values.

For example, a mother who believes strongly in the role of a full-time homemaker will choose not to work outside the home; a mother who believes in sharing the household finances will contribute through paid employment; and a mother who believes in providing a role model for her children in the world of work will take paid employment and will probably talk to her children about it.

What Kind of Mother Am I?

Like every other mum, I want to do my best for my children and set them a great example. And, like every other mum, I don't always

23

get it right – in fact far from it. I'm a bit of a perfectionist and I often fall short of my own standards. But I get up every morning determined to do my absolute best for them.

Sometimes I'm so caught up in the day-to-day whirlwind of childcare, work and finding a little bit of time for me and Richie that there doesn't seem to be a moment to sit down and think about what my values and beliefs are and the qualities I want to pass on to the girls. But it's so important to know yourself, and who you are as a mother. Inevitably perhaps, the girls will get some of my weaknesses along with, I hope, my strengths. But what are those strengths and weaknesses? Do I know myself well enough to assess them honestly? And can I make a conscious effort to develop more of what I'd like to pass on?

What my parents passed on to me, and I think to my brother and sister too, were strong and sound basic values about the way we live our lives. Things like honesty, reliability and loyalty, the importance of family and of living within your means. I didn't question any of these, they have always stood me in good stead and I hope I am able to pass them on to my girls.

When I was growing up, the world seemed like a safe place in which people were fundamentally good. But after I was attacked, for many weeks I lay in hospital, so badly injured that I was close to death. As I gradually recovered and endured dozens of operations to rebuild my face, I wondered if I would ever again be able to believe in the fundamental goodness of other people. The world seemed like a brutal and frightening place.

Until then, I had taken so much for granted. But at that point I had to make some decisions for myself. Would I give in to evil, or survive? Would I see the world as awful, or find a way to remember that it is beautiful too? Would I decide never to trust anyone again, or could I separate the people who didn't deserve my trust from those who did?

It was at that point that I took on some beliefs of my own. I chose to believe that what doesn't break us makes us stronger. And I believed in myself as a survivor because, in my fury at what had happened, I decided that I would not let the men who had injured me triumph. If I caved in, hid away or felt ashamed of how I looked, then I would be letting them win. And I definitely believed that you should not let those who wish you harm succeed.

These new beliefs, in my right to survive, in the possibility of rebuilding a life from the ruins of an old one, in the power to help others and to do good in the world, served me well. I worked, slowly and painstakingly, to recover and then to find a way forward – not easy since I had lost not just my health and looks but my home in London and my work modelling and presenting. And out of the ruins of my life, which caused me many moments of heartbreak, I found a way to make a new future for myself. I started the Katie Piper Foundation to help other burns survivors and, after the documentaries about what happened to me, I became a presenter, writer and public speaker. I wanted to be visible and present and to speak out, I would not hide away or feel less-than or ashamed. And that, I guess, defines the kind of mother I want to be, and hope I am.

Qualities

In the course of all of this, over the past ten years, I discovered I had qualities I hadn't known existed. Qualities I was proud to possess and which stood me in good stead. I discovered I had courage, determination and persistence. I also developed resilience; the ability to bounce back whenever I faced criticism, cruel and thoughtless comments or online trolling – and I had plenty of all of these. I had to decide not to let it get me down – after all, these people didn't even know me, and certainly had no idea what I had been through. So why should I let myself be affected by what they said? I focused instead on all the kindness, support and encouragement that came my way, not only from those who knew me, but from many who didn't and who chose to care.

I want to pass on to my girls all that I have learned. I don't want to be over-protective or to wrap them in cotton wool, because when you do that there's a danger of making them feel incapable of handling things for themselves. I would rather teach them how to handle life's knocks, so they feel empowered. When Belle was pushed over by another child at toddler group I wanted to leap in and cuddle her, but instead I let her get to her feet and waited to see whether she needed me or not. For a second, she seemed to be about to start yelling, but then she looked at me, smiling at her and saying, 'You're alright, Belle,' and she went back to her game. She didn't need me to overreact, she handled it and, even though she was under two at the time, she had learned a valuable lesson – that she could be pushed over and choose to get back up and carry on.

These are some of the most important qualities I would like my girls to have:

Kindness

If there's one thing that I believe should be a guiding principle in life it is to be kind. Being kind means being thoughtful, considerate, compassionate and understanding. It is not the same as being a pushover or always giving in. Sometimes standing firm can be the kindest thing to do.

Persistence

Most achievements are the result of persistence. You can have education and talent but if you don't know how to stick at something then all the education and talent in the world won't help you. Most great inventions, ideas, books and achievements are the result of persistence, often in the face of many failures. Just look at how a baby learns to walk – they fall down and get back up again and keep on trying until they can do it.

Resilience

If you are resilient you are tough, flexible and quick to recover from any setback. You can roll with the punches, laugh off an insult, see the bigger picture when something goes wrong. With resilience life's inevitable disasters – small or big – won't break you.

Confidence

With confidence you can ask for what you want and speak up when you have something to say. You believe in yourself and your

27

abilities. This isn't the same as being full of yourself or too big for your boots. It's an inner knowledge that you are OK, whatever you do, and that you deserve good things in life.

Can-do Attitude

I want the girls to have a 'can-do' attitude to life. Belle gets frustrated sometimes when she's trying to do something and can't quite manage it. I encourage her to keep trying, because it's useful to know that sometimes in life, especially as a woman, you have to work that bit harder and make people believe in you. Learning not to give up is character-building. We all have to do things when we're feeling ill, tired, nervous, and less able than someone else. Sticking with it and showing that you can do it anyway is so important.

Bravery

This is an important one and I'll come back to it again later on. Girls in our society (and most others) aren't encouraged to be physically brave. We tell girls to 'be careful', 'watch out', 'wait, it might be dangerous' and so on, many more times than we do boys. Girls are encouraged to be fearful, while boys are encouraged to be gutsier. This has to change – because if you are physically fearful, you will be fearful in all aspects of your life. The boy who learns to climb a wall on his own becomes the man who isn't afraid to speak out in a meeting, while the girl who believes she can't climb the wall without mum or dad holding her, becomes the woman who stays silent in the meeting, even though she has a great idea to put forward.

Girls are so often brought up to be timid and helpless and not to take physical risks. Yet small girls (pre-puberty) are mostly just as strong as small boys – there aren't so many physical differences. And they're certainly capable of being just as adventurous. So why do parents caution girls more than boys, help them (for instance with a climbing frame in the playground) more than boys and encourage them to hold back?

I want my girls to feel physically confident, on their bikes, on a climbing frame, on a playground ride and, when they get older, on a surfboard, a horse, a climbing wall or anything else they fancy having a go at because it will teach them to assess their own capabilities and to be resilient and confident.

EXERCISE:
THE PCP GRID

Educational psychologist Kairen Cullen introduced me to a simple exercise to help identify our most important beliefs and values, and the behaviour and qualities we draw from them. It's called the PCP (Personal Construct Psychology) grid and it's based on the theories of psychologist George Kelly, who first wrote about it back in the 1950s. He had three central ideas:

- Individuals have their own unique and personal beliefs about the world and themselves in the world, and they base the way they behave on these beliefs.
- Every person is constantly trying out different ways of

29

behaviour in order to meet their needs and to function effectively.

- Individuals' beliefs can be drawn out and understood through a particular way of questioning.

The exercise is very simple and doesn't take long:

1. Draw a grid, like the one below, with 4 rows and 12 columns.

Make the first and last columns wide enough to write a couple of words. Head the first column 'Emergent Qualities' and the last column 'Contrast Qualities'. Number the other columns from 1 to 10, going from right to left.

Emergent Qualities	10	9	8	7	6	5	4	3	2	1	Contrast Qualities

2. Now ask yourself, 'What kind of mother am I?' Without thinking about it for too long, list the first three words or phrases that come to mind in the first column on the left-hand side of the page. These are your emergent qualities.

3. Next, look at the three words or phrases you have written and for each one decide what word or phrase you would use to describe a person who was the opposite of the way you described yourself. Write these in the last column on the right-hand side. These are your contrast qualities.

4. Now rate yourself from 10 to 1 on each of the qualities.

Place an X on the grid for where you rate yourself for each of the three qualities.

5. Finally, place an O on the grid for where you would like to be for each of the three qualities.

You'll see what I mean from the grid below, which was filled in by Helen, a friend of mine.

This exercise is valuable because the truth is that we are rarely one pure quality. There is always a shadow side, which can become more obvious when life throws up obstacles and challenges. For example, when life is good, the kind, encouraging and available aspects of us are likely to come to the fore. However, say the family income suddenly reduces, someone gets ill or there's a bereavement, the shadow qualities may become more obvious.

Helen's PCP Grid

Emergent Qualities	10	9	8	7	6	5	4	3	2	1	Contrast Qualities
Very kind		X									
		O									
Encouraging		X									
		O									
Available		O				X					

Helen's Story

You can see from Helen's PCP grid above that Helen places a lot of importance on being kind, encouraging and available for her children.

She's mum to two girls, aged three and six, and she's also a part-time nurse at the local hospital (four eight-hour shifts a week). Her husband is a delivery driver and Helen's income is vital to the household finances. Her two-year-old, Daisy, is happy going to a trusted child-minder, while her six-year-old, Amy, goes home after school two days a week with a friend and her mum, who gives her tea. Her husband looks after the girls if she has a weekend shift.

Everything seemed fine with these arrangements – except that Helen felt guilty about being away from her girls so much. This was made a lot worse by the attitude of her in-laws, who were very critical of the fact that she was back at work with such young children. They also thought it put too much pressure on her husband who looks after the girls if Helen is working at the weekend and who takes Daisy to the child-minder and Amy to school when Helen has an early shift.

During Helen's maternity leave, when she had been at home all the time for the first year of each child's life, she had suffered from mild depression. This had lifted when she went back to work. Although her primary reason for working was the money, Helen actually loved her work and felt good about her job. When she thought about why she had wanted to be more available for her girls, Helen realized she meant emotional availability. She didn't feel she always needed to be physically present with the girls, but she did want to be available to listen and engage with them fully when they were together. This was something she could improve on without changing her working hours.

Helen and her husband, Dan, sat down and talked it through. He felt fine about her working and didn't mind doing his share of childcare. And he hadn't really been bothered by his parents' criticisms. But then, as Helen pointed out, they weren't directed at him.

Helen and Dan agreed that it was good for the girls to see their mum going out to work and enjoying her job and it was also good for them to see both parents sharing the financial and childcare responsibilities.

Dan agreed to be much more aware of his parents' criticisms and to stand up for Helen, and they also agreed to give his parents lots of reassurance that their grandchildren were safe and happy and being well cared for.

Changing Beliefs

Helen's story made me think about how beliefs can sometimes change through the generations. Her in-laws believed a mum should stay at home with young children. They're not alone in that, many people, especially in older generations, believe the same thing.

My own mum was at home with us when we were small. She

switched from teaching to child-minding so that she could be at home with us, and when she went back to teaching it was as a supply teacher, so that she could take time off to be with us whenever she needed to. And, of course, she was always around for the holidays.

For me, it was very different. My work isn't nearly so flexible – if I'm in the middle of recording a TV series I can't just stop, and I have talks and meetings in the diary that have been arranged weeks or even months in advance. And, like Helen, I need to work to help support the family and I love what I do. I feel lucky to have work and I don't want to stop.

I'm also very lucky to have great childcare in place, but that doesn't stop me feeling guilty sometimes, and sad at missing time with the girls, when they're changing so fast and learning all kinds of new things every day.

My mum felt a bit uneasy at first about me having childcare. Her own parents had a live-in nanny and she spent very little time with them. That contributed to her decision to stay at home with us when we were small. I had to reassure her that I planned to spend all the time I could with the girls and that Richie would also be around for them a lot, just as my dad was for us. We just needed childcare for when Richie and I were both out at work. For me, having childcare is a support for us as parents, not a substitute for us. The good thing about my type of job is that although I do have to work long hours that take me away from family life, sometimes I can have days and even weeks at home with them, to make up for those times when I am away filming.

The girls were fine as well. They have a lovely carer and they accept, very happily, when Mummy has to go to work, just as Daddy does. Mum saw how necessary it was for us, like so many other working couples, and that far from being a bad thing, an extra adult in the girls' world has meant someone else to have fun with.

I was touched when Mum told me, in a quiet moment, that she was so happy for me to have the work opportunities I have had, after the years of being ill and undergoing treatment. And she admitted that, much as she loved being a stay-at-home mum, she might have enjoyed more opportunities to try new things outside the home.

Rules

One thing Mum and I really do agree on is the need for clear and simple rules. Your children need to know who is in charge – and that needs to be you.

There are several reasons to have rules that everyone in the house knows and lives by:

- Too much power is actually frightening for children; they need to know who is in charge and that it's not them. Rules reassure them and make them feel safe.
- Rules can make children feel good and competent. For instance, the rule that we all help with setting the table and clearing up.
- Rules help prepare children for life – the world is full of rules they will have to follow.

- If you have rules you sometimes keep and sometimes break, it's unpredictable, and that's frightening too.

Rules always need to make sense, and to make everyone's life easier. Take bedtime, for instance. If the rule is that bedtime is 7pm for a four-year-old, then they know what to expect and we know that they will get enough sleep, since four-year-olds are always awake at the crack of dawn. We also know that we'll get a bit of adult downtime! A bedtime routine, like bath, drink, story, helps them to wind down and prepare for bed, and we all enjoy it. I've seen kids who are allowed to stay up until they 'feel tired' and they're grumpy and miserable. We know how much sleep children need – they don't.

It's the same thing with eating – we know what's good for them, they don't. So, having to eat fruit and vegetables is a rule, and so is a limit on sugary things and no sugary teeth-rotting drinks. It just makes sense to give them the best shot possible at good health.

Other rules, like saying sorry when you hurt someone, not shouting at people and waiting your turn, fit around our beliefs and values. Belle recently went through a phase of shouting at us when she got frustrated. I would say to her, 'No-one else shouts in this house, I don't want you to either.' She had to stop and think for a minute and then she nodded. She knew that we don't shout at each other in our house.

It isn't always easy sticking to rules, especially when you have a small face looking at you angelically and pleading for 'just five more minutes' or 'just one more sweet'. And it can be especially hard if you are a single parent. With two parents they can – and should – back one another up; no turning to Dad because Mum said no. But on your own you have to do it alone, reminding yourself why you have rules and reinforcing yourself. Calling a friend can help, but they aren't there in the moment when you are negotiating with a child. The only thing that helps is remembering that the child depends on you to show them how the world works, and to make their world safe and reliable.

Choices

Having clear rules doesn't exclude making choices. In fact, I tell Belle (and will tell Penelope when she's old enough) that you always have a choice. It's a great thing to teach children from the start, as long as you keep the choice simple – for instance, do you want the apple or the banana? Or do you want to play with Lego or the train?

There can be choices about behaviour too. Take Belle's fake crying, as we have come to call it in our family. She's brilliant at it and for a while she was doing it all the time. If she didn't get her own way, she would start wailing and she could even sprout a few tears if a command performance was needed. Clearly a budding actress!

The thing is, I know her too well. I can spot the fake crying and I call her out on it. One morning she appeared in our bedroom at 4am, asking to get into our bed with us. I told her to go back to bed and she started wailing. I said, 'Belle, that's fake crying,' and she stopped and said, 'Yeah, it is,' and went back to bed.

In the end, we started a sticker chart to reward her for every day she gets through with no fake crying. After a while, she would come home and say, 'I did fake crying at school today.' She knew the difference and she knew that fake crying was not going to get our attention.

She had the choice: fake-cry, or earn a sticker and put it towards a reward.

Sticker charts are great for monitoring positive progress and encouraging self-reliant behaviours.

Belle's still very small, but she's already doing a few jobs around the house – picking up her toys and puzzles (before the dog chews them) and helping with practical things like bed-making and washing up.

We encourage her to do as much as possible for herself and try not to do things for her that she can manage on her own. Like putting on socks and shoes. At three she could do it, but she could also take half an hour over it when I had ten minutes to get her out of the door. So encouraging self-reliance does, sometimes, have to be time-dependent!

Role Models

We all have role models as we grow up, whether we know it or not. Sometimes we're not conscious of modelling ourselves on someone else, and sometimes we are. But the important thing is that we do it, and we continue to do it over and over again throughout our lives.

Children have lots of role models; some are real people around them that they know, some are real but they don't personally know them and some are virtual. When they're small, there are the role models so many children love; superheroes like Spiderman and Disney princesses like *Frozen*'s Elsa or *Aladdin*'s Jasmine. And when they get bigger the role models tend to be pop stars, adventurers, animal experts or actors. Like it or not, millions of teenage girls love the Kardashians, Justin Bieber and Miley Cyrus.

All these role models influence the attitudes, behaviour and choices that children and teenagers make. So it's worth taking time to look at your child's role models to see who they are, what they represent and what they are teaching. But, although at first glance some role models seem obviously bad and others good, it isn't always that simple – some of the 'bad' ones still have useful and worthwhile lessons to teach.

The first and most important role model is, of course, you. As a mother, you are the most significant and most influential example for your daughter. From the moment, as a small baby, she smiles in response to your smile, she will be copying what you say and do, whether consciously or not. And she will learn from you what it is to be a woman.

I decided to find out a bit more about the importance of role models, to prepare myself for when Belle and Penelope began to choose their heroes and heroines.

The Value of Role Models

Good role models can provide real-life examples of how to manage life's challenges and difficulties with courage and humour. They can also provide examples of ways to work, to achieve goals and to solve problems. This kind of role model can be invaluable for a growing child.

When a good role model demonstrates, for instance, how to deal firmly and confidently with someone being rude in a shop, or someone in the street demanding money, then a child who sees this will take in the behaviour – much of it unconsciously – and begin to model it.

No matter how good you are as a parent you can't be and do

everything for your child. It's a good idea for all parents to choose 'extra' adults to be in their children's lives – friends and relatives who will spend time with the child, have fun with them, help them with difficulties and provide a great example.

Ideally, you should choose a couple of role models for your child – people you like and trust, who will agree to be consistently in your child's life. But there will also be role models who your child chooses, in their lives or, more likely, online, who you feel might not be so good for them. And then it's important to know how damaging the 'wrong' role model can be and how to handle it.

Mum Comes First

As a small girl, your daughter will want to be just like you. As a teenager, she may think she wants to be completely different from you, but she will already have learned so much from you. And later on, as an adult, she may be glad that she's so like you.

Mothers tend to follow one of two patterns. They either repeat the way in which their own mothers went about things, or they base what they do on what they consider to be a completely different style.

In the end, most mothers combine the two, finding their own style, with some elements that are just like their own mothers and some that are very different.

No matter how lovely your own mother was and how close you were, there will always be a few things that you'll want to do differently. But just remember, that means your daughter won't think you did a perfect job either!

We mums want to get it right for our daughters, but we're

human, we mess up, have bad days and make mistakes. Being a good role model is as much about how you handle these things as it is about the way you live your life and the choices you make.

In an ideal world, mothers as role models would provide consistent living examples of:

- Good self-esteem and confidence
- The ability to problem-solve
- The capacity to manage stress and/or adversity
- Good communication skills
- Positive and reciprocal relationships
- How to be healthy and fit

Not many of us feel we can easily model all these things, no matter how much we'd love to. But what we can do is be aware of our strengths, use them and at the same time work on the areas where we're not so strong.

What Kind of Role Model Am I?

Like most teenagers, I followed pop stars, actors and models I thought were cool. But there's no doubt that my most important role model was my mum. Her patience and warmth showed me what it was to love and be loved. She was always calm; she didn't shout or get angry, so I grew up feeling that the world was very safe. And she and Dad were a brilliant example of sharing childcare and responsibilities in the house: they both did their share equally, there were no 'mum' jobs and 'dad' jobs.

I'd like to be an equally good role model for Belle and Penelope, but my world is very different from the way Mum's was when I was young. I go out to work, I am not always around and I have a lot of demands on my time to juggle along with being there for my girls. I don't think that's a bad thing, I want them to be able to support themselves and be independent, so showing them what it is to be a working mother is important. I know I don't always get things right. Sometimes I'm a great model for the 'mum who spends too much time on her phone' or the 'mum who is rushing out of the door' or the 'mum who tries to fit too many things into her day'. But – while managing my time is always a work in progress – I don't think it's a bad thing for them to see me under pressure, as long as I also show them how to manage that pressure by prioritizing, saying no to things that are less important and being there for them when it matters.

And I know I can be a good mum, and a good role model, in lots of ways that matter. I'm not vain or obsessed with looks – I let go of all of that after the attack. Not just because I lost the looks I had, but because it made me realize that what matters is not what's on the surface but what lies underneath, the essential you, the heart and head and spirit of who you are. I want to teach the girls this from the start, so that they never get too obsessed with their appearance.

I'm also thoughtful and caring towards the people I love, I care deeply about justice in the world and I try always to look for ways to make the world a better place and to help others.

Like so many other mums, I juggle work and the family, business meetings with cleaning the bathroom, bedtime stories with

43

sending emails. But I do make sure that I have quality time with the girls, when I can listen to them, play with them and enjoy them and when they know that their mum is completely theirs.

I talk to them all the time and I hope the communication channels will always stay open and that they'll always feel able to bring problems or worries to me as well as sharing fun things.

I hope that, by refusing to let my attackers win, I will be showing my daughters what it is to stand up for yourself, to fight back in positive ways and to be brave.

I hope I will teach them how to make good choices, in life and relationships and work. Most importantly, I will tell them there is always a choice about whatever you do. Bad things happen in life, I can't hide that from them, but I can help them find ways to cope, to recover and to look for the value in everything.

Family and Friends as Role Models

As children grow a little older and more involved with others in the family, they take on other role models. And the older they get, the wider their circle of role models becomes.

Grandmothers, aunties and cousins can all become role models and this is a good thing, because children will learn something from everyone.

Once a child is at school, teachers often provide role models. Many of us had a favourite teacher we tried hard to please, whose approval meant so much and who seemed like the kindest person in the world. And alongside teachers, there may be other authority figures – the scout leader, the dance or gym instructor, the babysitter.

As the circle widens, what these people teach the child will be layered on what she has already learned from her mum. It all adds to the rich complexity of each of us as we grow up. So, encouraging your daughter to befriend and learn from other people – ones you like and trust – is a good thing. They need to learn that everything doesn't revolve around you, and that they can go off with someone else, have a good time and come back to you.

Sometimes, this can be a bit tough though. When your daughter suddenly looks up to someone else, having worshipped only you for the first few years, you have to learn to deal with it and let go, as Kathy and Gemma's story shows.

Kathy and Gemma's Story

Gemma adored her mother's sister Laura from a very early age. But Kathy, her mum, was concerned about the influence Laura had over Gemma, as she and her sister were so very different and had entirely different lifestyles. Kathy had worked hard at school, gone to university to study medicine and then combined her career as a GP with having her own family. Laura, on the other hand, left school at sixteen, did many different jobs and then became a modestly successful actress. The original party animal, Laura was twice married and divorced, had a string of different partners, smoked and drank, and vowed she would never have children. However, she loved Gemma to bits, heaped presents and attention on her and, as her niece grew older, Laura often asked Kathy whether Gemma could stay with her.

Kathy managed to confine Gemma's time with her aunt to the occasional Saturday night, but when Gemma was ten Laura invited her on a holiday to the West Indies for two weeks. Gemma was desperate to go, but Kathy said no. Laura was deeply upset and the sisters rowed and then stopped speaking to one another. Gemma, devastated and furious with her mum, became moody and aggressive.

Kathy agonized over whether she had done the right thing. She was a single parent and, while she was on good terms with her ex-husband (who thought she should say yes and couldn't see what the problem was), she needed someone to talk the whole thing over with. So she went to see her oldest friend, Jo, who helped her to see, over a long chat and several cups of tea, that what Kathy really feared, more than the influence of Laura's lifestyle, was the idea of being replaced by her sister in her daughter's affections. 'That's not going to happen,' Jo assured her. 'Laura is special and exciting to Gemma, but you're the centre of her world.' Kathy knew that what Jo said was true, she had listened to her own insecurity rather than the strong and confident knowledge that Gemma loved her and always would.

Kathy arranged to meet Laura and she apologized for reacting so harshly and explained her worries about Laura's lifestyle. Laura, in turn, explained that she wanted to spend the holiday caring for her niece as well as Kathy did, and that it would give her a chance to experience being like a mother for a short time, as she knew she would never actually be a mum. The sisters were reconciled, and Kathy and Laura agreed some basic ground rules for the trip. Gemma was thrilled that the holiday was going ahead and it proved to be a great success – Gemma and Laura had a wonderful time and Kathy, knowing she would miss Gemma, planned a few treats and nights out to take advantage of the extra time on her hands. To her surprise, she loved catching up with friends, going for a couple of long walks and watching a box-set or two with a tub of ice cream.

By the time Gemma came home, thrilled to be back with her mum, all three of them had benefited. Gemma had a loving auntie as an extra role model, Laura had loved looking after Gemma but was happy to get back to her single lifestyle, and Kathy had enjoyed the break more than she had ever imagined she would.

This story really sums up many of the blessings of encouraging your daughter to find role models within your network of extended family and friends. It broadens your child's world, allowing them, and their role models, to have rich and nourishing relationships, and it gives you a chance to shift your perspective a little, and to remind yourself of the person you were before you became a mum.

Diane Says:

Katie's first role model, other than me, was her older brother Paul. She always wanted to play with him and do whatever he was doing. She wanted to emulate him, but she put her own slant on it, so when he did karate, she did judo . . . He joined the Cubs so she joined the Brownies . . . He did football, she did gymnastics. Paul had the Spiderman, Superman and He-Man costumes, and Katie used to dress up as She-Ra (Princess of Power, the twin sister of He-Man) and play-fight with him.

She had Barbie dolls too. Looking back, Barbie was probably an awful role model, with her impossibly long legs, long blonde hair and tiny waist, although at least there was Dr Barbie, Teacher Barbie, Businesswoman Barbie and so on, so she did work. I thought Katie wouldn't approve of the stereotyping, so I had to tease her when she told me that Belle loved Barbie dolls and already had quite a few!

In school, there were teachers Katie looked up to. Mrs C, a teacher in the junior school had a reputation for being a bit fierce but the children loved her because she was firm but fair and expected high standards from her pupils. Katie once told me, 'I am so scared of Mrs C – if she ever spoke to me I would faint!' I used to do supply work in the same school so I told Mrs C about this. One lunchtime Mrs C came into the staffroom laughing and said to me, 'Well, I've just spoken to your daughter and she managed not to faint.' I still smile when I think about that! In secondary school, there were also some teachers who inspired and motivated Katie, just as good teachers should. Her English teacher and her drama teacher both saw her potential and I think that's why she enjoyed those subjects.

As Katie grew up, she developed a social conscience. She admired those who campaigned on behalf of the less fortunate, particularly animals, and on a few occasions she would get together with her friends and organize fundraising events like cake sales and jumble sales. She is even wearing a Save the Whale badge in one of her school photos. She also wanted to save gorillas, horses and donkeys.

When Katie became a teenager, she got into music. She loved listening to Michael Jackson (she still does) and she also liked the Spice Girls. One of her party pieces at Christmas was enlisting her sister Suzy and her cousin to dress up as the Spice Girls and sing their songs at the top of their voices. So 'Girl Power' was a phrase she was quite familiar with.

I believe Katie will be a fantastic role model for Belle. She already encourages Belle to form her own opinions, she talks to her about everything, she asks her questions and she explains things to her. Belle will grow up with a mum who has a strong work ethic, who values her home and family and is determined to lead a fulfilling life.

Fantasy Role Models

Alongside the known and familiar role models, most children have what I think of as fantasy role models. These differ, according to the child's age. When they're younger, they tend to love characters from cartoons, Disney and superhero films and stories. When they get a bit older, they are likely to get more excited about pop stars, models, actresses and sometimes people just famous for being famous.

A lot of parents quake at this, including me. Many of these figures are one-dimensional – they don't do anything useful, they are obsessed with looks and surrounded by hype and not who we want our children to look up to. I've met plenty of women who are completely obsessed with their looks and they're not great company. And the biggest danger of fantasy role models is that they appear 'perfect' while us mere mortals are not.

But does it actually harm our kids to want to follow the activities of role models like this?

The Disney Princess

Girls and boys tend to be directed towards role models that adults assume they will want to emulate. And so, while boys might want to mimic Spiderman (my friend's son, aged four, insisted on wearing his Spiderman costume, day and night, for two months), girls' heroines are often Disney princesses.

At first glance, this might seem worrying. In today's age, with women running companies and striving towards equality in all areas of life , why are little girls still dressing up in frothy dresses and tiaras and idolizing princesses who sit around waiting for the right prince?

Look twice, though, and you realize that Disney princesses have changed over the years. Snow White might have run around after a bunch of small men and waited years for her prince, but the modern princesses are a lot feistier, and they have plenty of characteristics that we might want girls to imitate.

The newer Disney princesses have determination, compassion, ambition and fearlessness. So much so that the England women's football team believes the traits of Disney princesses are exactly what you need to become a successful player. In 2017, the Football Association joined with Disney on a campaign that focused on Disney princesses' strong attributes to encourage more young females into football.

Captain Steph Houghton said, 'Being brave, being strong and being kind are all important attributes when it comes to building a successful team. They're all qualities that girls can learn from Disney princesses.'

Disney has definitely moved on from the more demure and delicate princesses of the past.

All the modern princesses have to strive to get where they want to be. They don't give up, they work hard and they have positive and determined attitudes. Mulan showed that women could fight just as well as men, if not better, and Merida, in the film *Brave*, showed an amazing adventurous spirit. As for Moana, in 2016, she had a far more realistic body type than her predecessors and – for the first time – there was no love interest. Instead of waiting for a prince, Moana was brave and daring and she set out to save her people.

There's more ethnic diversity among the princesses these days too, a definite move in the right direction, with Tiana, the first black princess, appearing in *The Princess and the Frog* in 2009. Moana was Polynesian and Pocahontas and Mulan were also women of colour.

Suzie Longstaff, headteacher of Putney High School, a girls' school in southwest London, has held assemblies about empowering girls through Disney princesses. 'My two children have grown up with Elsa and Anna and Moana and Ariel. They are all so much better female role models.'

In 2016, Disney launched a ten-point checklist of what it takes to be one of their princesses.

And it's pretty good – I'd be happy for my daughters to take these messages on board.

1. Care for others
2. Live healthily
3. Don't judge a book by its cover
4. Be honest
5. Be a friend you can trust
6. Believe in yourself
7. Right wrongs
8. Try your best
9. Be loyal
10. Never give up

Disney is aiming to keep up with the times. There's still a way to go, but it's reassuring for mums whose daughters wear Disney outfits and worship their heroines, to know that there is plenty of positive reinforcement coming across through the characters.

The Reality-TV Star

Most of us would like our daughters to move on pretty quickly from Disney princesses to a wider, more diverse set of role models.

And by the end of primary school, they have usually left Disney behind. But while we hope they will then be entranced by the work of scientists, animal experts, company leaders and entrepreneurs, all too often we find them following beauty bloggers, actors and the Kardashians – a family famous for absolutely nothing and yet who take up infinite amounts of space on the internet and in newspapers and magazines.

So, should we worry when this happens?

Since we're on the subject of the Kardashians, let's take Kim – voluptuous role model for millions of young girls, married to singer Kanye West, mother to children named North and Saint, and star of Instagram and Twitter. Is Kim a bad influence?

Kim is all about her body; her anatomy is dissected and discussed endlessly. She puts hundreds photos of herself online and talks about what she is eating, drinking, doing non-stop, and most of it is pretty dull. And she says that she doesn't leave the house without an hour-and-a-half long beauty routine. Not a habit you want to encourage.

On the other hand, it can be argued that Kim flaunts her assets with confidence. She isn't a skinny size zero model shape at all; she's curvy, with a well-rounded bottom she likes to show off. She trains hard, wears clothes that flatter her and gives off a lot of body confidence.

Kim also tweets for causes – encouraging her followers to give blood, support gun control, and donate clothes to charity to raise funds. So, she's not all bad news.

The bottom line is that many girls will follow Kim and other role models we might think of as undesirable, because their friends do

53

it. Children want to be part of the group, accepted by their peers, so they'll tend to do the same things. That doesn't necessarily mean they will swallow wholesale the mantra that 'you are as you look'. No matter how devoted they seem to Kim etc., they have many other influences, and primary among them is you.

Talk About Role Models

Whichever star or character your daughter chooses to follow – and she will choose, because even if you do your best to steer her away from the ones you dislike, she'll hear about them through school friends – the most important thing is that you keep talking to her about it.

I don't mean a serious 'we need to talk about this' conversation or a dismissive 'that person is a waste of time', because if you come down too heavily your daughter may still worship whoever you disapprove of, she just won't tell you about it. Or the two of you will end up in conflict. Either way, you probably won't convince her to drop her current idol.

So, talk to her without criticism or judgement. Here are some suggested guidelines:

- Ask her, with an open mind, why she likes person (or character) A.
- Discuss A's characteristics, positive and negative. Your daughter may not think there are negatives, so get round to them gently, in a thoughtful way.
- Ask your daughter questions about all the characteristics

you discuss. For instance, why do you think A does that? What do you think A could do differently?

- Don't talk down to her. A child who feels dismissed or patronized will clam up. Yes, you do know more than she does, but it just doesn't work to be heavy-handed.
- Tell her what figures you liked when you were younger, and why (and not just the 'good' ones, be honest). She needs to know she's normal. Having a crush on a star is a rite of passage.

Talking is the key to so much. So keep the communication lines open. Talk about life, the news, school, society, friends and family, and let role models simply be a part of that ongoing conversation.

When Role Models Mess Up

The Disney princesses always come out on top. Their paths are carefully charted. But for the more human role models your child might pick – the music stars, the reality stars – life can be very different. Lots of them mess up. We hear about drunken episodes, drug addictions, public embarrassment, broken relationships and more. And being able to discuss your children's role models is especially important when those role models mess up.

So, what do you say when you see a photograph of your child's once picture-perfect role model looking wrecked or dressed in little more than a dishcloth or weeping mascara down her face because her boyfriend left her?

Sometimes, celebrities attract headlines in such a negative fashion that it can be hard to explain their wild antics to kids who've looked up to them.

Let's take Miley Cyrus as an example. This once squeaky-clean star came to mega-stardom at the age of fourteen as Hannah Montana, acting alongside her dad in the story of an ordinary girl who lives a double life as a famous pop singer. The series transformed Miley into a real-life pop princess. So far so good. But then, in 2013, at the age of twenty-one, Miley decided to shake off her schoolgirl image by wearing nothing but a latex skin-coloured bra and pants while singing at the MTV Video Music Awards. She also behaved in a very sexually provocative manner, draping herself over a male singer, flicking out her tongue and writhing seductively before touching herself suggestively with an outsized foam hand. Not good, given that her fan base had an average age of ten.

Many of her fans described the performance, on Twitter, as embarrassing and disturbing. Miley later admitted that it wasn't her best move and said, with impressive understatement, 'I don't have a normal life.' Meanwhile, millions of parents had the job of explaining what it was all about to their children.

An episode like that can be confusing for a child, but it's a great opportunity for your daughter to develop her critical powers. Discussing it along the lines of, 'Why do you think she did it?' 'How do you think she felt when she received so much criticism?' is a good start. You don't have to hide your own feelings, but express them moderately. If you slam into Miley, your daughter will defend her, and that's not the outcome you want.

Ask your daughter (depending on her age) if she understands

what happened and what she thinks the problem is with, for instance, giving a performance like Miley's. And talk about the consequences – the criticisms, the possible loss of endorsements and so on (just as your child gets consequences when she does something wrong). It's a chance to talk about what it means to make poor decisions and a great opportunity to say that we all mess up sometimes, by making mistakes or bad decisions, and that stars simply do it more publicly. You can point out the downside of fame; that everyone sees when you get it wrong, and that most stars who mess up do sort themselves out and go on to apologize or talk about what happened with regret.

The most important aspect of messing up is how we deal with it afterwards, and this can lead to a valuable conversation with your daughter. What do you do after messing up? You can learn from it, say sorry, put things right if possible and make a different choice next time.

Episodes like this become teachable moments, if you handle them with care. The conversation can provide an opportunity to go on to talk about your child's worries, what people at school do (and think) and the pressures of life.

Finding Meaning in Life

The honest truth, as many studies prove, is that meaning in life is found not in excitement and stardom, success and glamour, but in what we do every day – work, relationships, friends, family. And this is what I want for my daughters – a life led with meaning and purpose.

Research shows that adolescents who do household chores feel a stronger sense of purpose. They might scoff at this, but it's because they're making a contribution to something bigger than themselves – the family.

Another study found that cheering up a friend was an activity that created meaning in a young person's life. Because it's our exchanges and relationships and productive pursuits that give us meaning.

Work contributes a lot of meaning to life, and I hope very much that my girls will find work they love, regardless of what it earns them financially. I don't mind whether they go to university or leave school at sixteen, as long as they do something that motivates them to get up each day, looking forward to work.

For me, meaningful work involves making a contribution to society, whether that is by advising people, supporting them or working together with them on a bigger project. I hope this is what my girls will discover for themselves.

I will always tell them that you don't have to be famous or change the world, in fact the famous often struggle because they have a false reality to live up to and they lose track of who they really are. Much better to pursue your interests and passions and find your own route to meaning.

As the girls get older, I'll talk to them about what really fires them up. It could be dance, maths, sport, travel, business – so many things. I'll give them lots of opportunities to try all kinds of different things to find out what they really love. And whatever their life choices, I want them to be self-sufficient and independent.

Ultimately, if a child's life is full and meaningful, if they can talk to you about what is going on in their world, then a few slightly less than ideal role models won't make any difference. They will still turn out to be well-rounded, capable women.

CHAPTER 4

Other Mums

Friends enrich every stage of our lives, but friendships during motherhood can be the difference between sinking and swimming, as you navigate the early days of the strange, unfamiliar territory that is being a new parent. So, in this chapter, I'm going to stray a little from the mothers and daughters theme and just concentrate on mums, because the connections and friendships we make as mothers, especially first-time mothers, are so important.

Suddenly life is utterly different and it revolves around a tiny person with seemingly endless needs. It doesn't matter what you were doing before you had baby – running your own company, taking part in Olympic-level races or managing a staff of hundreds – afterwards you can find just navigating the eat-wind-sleep-eat again routine completely daunting and you feel as though you're never quite on top of things and never sure if you're doing it right. Life as you knew it has changed completely.

It's easy to underestimate the challenges of early parenthood. Loneliness and isolation are often a part of it, as you find yourself unable to get out of the front door, or even into your clothes, for days at a time. It's easy to feel a bit lost at this stage – how come no-one told you, or prepared you for such a huge change? Almost overnight you don't even feel like the same person you were before.

The friends you had pre-baby, while lovely and supportive, just can't understand what it feels like. You're lucky, you have a gorgeous baby, everything is perfect – so you shouldn't feel like a walking zombie covered with baby sick, or like someone who used to be able to manage several things at once but now can't even feed one small person without one or both of you ending up in tears.

This is where motherhood friendships really come into their own. What you need, to keep you sane, to remind you that there is a funny side and to listen when you complain, are other mothers. Anyone who is going through it too will share the pain and the joy in a way that no-one else can.

You may be lucky enough to have an old friend, or even friends, who become parents at the same time. But that's not always the case. And for the rest of us who haven't got good friends going through it too, the answer is finding new friends. Not something that feels easy when you have your hands full of soggy nappies, but actually there are lots of ways to make friends with other mothers. What's more, this isn't something that you should look on as optional – it's a necessity.

The friends you make when your child is small get to know the new you – the post-baby person you feel you're only just getting to know too. Because when you have a baby your identity undergoes a massive shift. You're a mother now and that's a whole different world from anything you were pre-baby. Parenthood is a journey and you need friends who will go along for the ride.

This is also the right time to decide that your whole life is not going to revolve around your child. That won't do her, or you, any good. She'll grow up selfish and you'll be lonely and resentful. So, make the decision that you have needs and rights too, and friends are right up there at the top of the list.

Why We Need Other Mums

New research suggests that having a baby can widen your social circle. And the new friends you make while pregnant, or after having your baby, can make a huge difference to your life. Many women find it easier to bond with other women at this stage – there's so much instantly in common, as you compare notes on how to get your baby sleeping through the night or how to wean them onto solids.

Friends made further down the line are the same. Whether it's at playgroup, school or after-school activities, fellow mums share the same concerns and joys and tend to love swapping tips and ideas. You remind one another of life before you had babies and support one another through the minefield of your offspring's early childhood.

A lot of new mothers worry about boring their old friends with endless baby talk. I've seen non-mum friends' eyes glaze over as I waxed lyrical about babygrows and nappies. To them, it's just not very interesting, while to you there is nothing on earth, right at that moment, more interesting. One friend, looking in wonder at my unwashed hair and milk-stained T-shirt, said, 'Don't babies sleep for about eighteen hours a day?' I wanted to say something unrepeatable. And yet she was, broadly speaking, right. If you haven't been there, then the rigmarole of new-baby life just doesn't make sense. That's why, for so many women, giving birth means bonding with your baby and with new friends too. I don't mean that you need to lose the old ones; just that it's harder for them to share this particular journey with you.

If you have extended family nearby, with mums, grandparents, aunts and cousins to help you, that can make a huge difference. But less than a third of new mothers do live near family, so we tend to rely on friends.

Feeling lonely and isolated after having a baby isn't unusual. Figures show that more than a quarter of new mums feel this way. When you have a baby you lose a lot too – your old way of life, your job (at least for a while) and your old way of spending time with friends. That's why meeting other mothers is so important.

Research has shown how important friendships are to our mental as well as our physical health. And in times of stress (and having a baby is a time of stress, without question), women don't simply opt for 'fight or flight' – as decades of research about men's reaction to stress has suggested; instead, they lean heavily on social support from friends. And that means in person, not on social media. There is no substitute for being able to chat to another mum about how you're feeling. So, while getting together with friends can seem like a luxury, in truth it's an emotional necessity.

The benefits of connecting with other mums include:

- Reducing isolation
- Companionship
- Finding a group of peers with whom to problem-solve, find solutions and give reassurance
- Offering and receiving practical support
- Supporting your identity as a mum, by highlighting the common ground and also the unique differences
- Learning new skills and accessing new knowledge in relation to mothering

Mums are never short of conversation material, so it's easy enough to join in. One survey found that sharing birth experiences was by far the most popular topic of conversation for new mums – after all, who else is going to listen spellbound to your tales of eighteen-hour labours and post-birth stitches.

New mums also talk about things like sleepless nights, baby ailments, being a good enough mum, whether to go back to work and the ups and downs of a post-baby sex life. They help one another through the baby blues, look after one another's children and help to keep one another sane.

Yasmin's Story

Yasmin was thirty when she had her first baby. She left her job as a section manager in a large department store a month before the birth and took a year's maternity leave. She and her husband Maz couldn't wait to become parents and they were thrilled when their daughter Malia was born.

After a week, Maz went back to his job as an aircraft engineer. And within a couple of weeks Yasmin, still recovering from a gruelling birth and grappling with the demands of a new baby, began to feel very down.

'It was so strange,' she says. 'I should have felt wonderful, but I didn't. No doubt hormones were still racing around in my body, I would feel good one minute and desolate the next. But more than anything I felt alone. Suddenly I was responsible for this small girl, and while I loved her, I didn't really know her yet. I had thousands of questions and no-one to answer them. Yes, I could look things up on websites, but that wasn't the same as being able to talk to someone kind and sympathetic face to face. None of my friends had babies at the same time. My best friend would call me, but she wanted to talk about what was happening at work and her new boyfriend, not cracked nipples and nappies.'

Yasmin had no idea how to meet other new mothers, until her health visitor mentioned a local mothers' circle. She gave Yasmin the number of one of the organizers, Sandi, and, after looking at the piece of paper sitting on the kitchen counter for a week, Yasmin called her.

Sandi was warm and friendly and she invited Yasmin along to the next meeting.

Three days later, Yasmin wheeled Malia's pram round to Sandi's house, where the meeting was being held. There were six mothers there and they all put their babies in the middle of the floor, keeping an eye on them while chatting to one another.

Shy at first, Yasmin was soon drawn into the circle. 'One mum asked me about Malia's birth and we were soon chatting,' she says. The two hours passed so fast and I went home feeling lighter and happier than I had since Maz went back to work. After that, I went along to the mums' circle every week. It was an absolute lifeline for me.'

O-T-H-E-R M-U-M-S

This mnemonic is a lovely way of summing up the value of other mothers:

Other mums show many different ways of being a mother

Talk to a range of other mums and find others on a similar wavelength

Help other mums as you would like to be helped

Each mother has her strengths, weak spots and challenges

Respect the differences in other mothering styles and their situations and resources

Make time for building and enjoying friendship with other mums

Use professional sources of support, such as GP, health visitor and school staff where *your* needs warrant this

Measure your mothering against your own value system and the wellbeing of yourself and your children. Try not to compare yourself unfavourably to others

Self-concept, self-esteem and self-knowledge as a mum can all be supported and challenged by other mums

Mums in My Life

I remember when a good friend of mine had her first baby. I was still in recovery after the attack and very preoccupied with everything in my world and I just didn't get how much her world had changed. I would talk about my stuff and I didn't really listen to her – I guess I wasn't sure, at that stage, whether I would ever be a mum so it all seemed very distant to me. She was such a good friend that she put up with me. It was only when I had Belle that I understood what a huge life change having a baby is. I felt bad for being so self-focused and not understanding, but thankfully we are still good friends.

When I had Belle, I do remember those strange early days when, alone with the baby at home, I felt everything had changed – my body, my life, my priorities – it all felt so unfamiliar and I was quite lonely. I couldn't take a lot of time off work because I was in the middle of filming a series, so I didn't really have time to make mum friends.

So much changed for me after the attack. I used to have lots of friends, I was incredibly sociable. But afterwards I became more wary, more anxious and I found contact with people quite a challenge. So it took me a while to make parent friends.

When Belle was two, I found a lovely group of mums at her ballet classes. When it first started, it was 'Mummy and Me' ballet and the children sat on your knee in a circle. It was the one club I tried to take time off to go to each week. There were seven or eight other mothers, all of them friendly and down-to-earth and I really enjoyed chatting to them.

When the girls were three, they were old enough to be dropped off at the class while us mums sat in the coffee shop nearby. I really enjoyed hearing about their lives. There was a real mix of mothers, some parenting full time, others back at work part time. It always strikes me that between them they have such a lot of knowledge, especially of the local area, the schools and so on. It's fantastically useful but, most of all, it's just fun to hang out with mums at the same stage.

How to Meet Other Mums

Many new mothers meet others during the pregnancy and antenatal period – that time before the birth when you start going to antenatal classes and check-ups and bumping into other mums-to-be doing the same.

Once you're at home caring for a newborn, you can start to tap into local mother and baby groups run by local health clinics, community and church groups. The National Childbirth Trust (NCT) offers a huge network of local groups across the country, with regular meet-ups for parents and their young children.

Later, when playgroup, nursery and formal school begin, the time before and after school and at parent/school events can offer opportunities to connect with others. And, of course, as the children begin to make friends with other children, they usually want to invite them home to tea or to shared activities and this provides another focal point for mums to meet.

Figures show that nearly half of new mums made friends with other women at mother and toddler groups, thirty per cent in antenatal classes and a fifth through other friends. And once a child reaches school age, the average mum's circle of friends increases by another five people.

Here are some of the opportunities to look out for:

- Antenatal classes
- Breastfeeding groups
- Parenting organizations such as the National Childbirth Trust
- Single-parent groups such as Gingerbread
- Children's activities – gym, ballet, brownies, sports clubs and so on
- The school gates – a great 'get-to-know you' spot
- Parenting websites, such as mumsnet.com – they can be a way to find out about events in your area and arrange to meet mums at similar life stages
- Local groups – look online

For those mums who continue with work outside home, the opportunities for meeting other mums are going to be fewer but it's still possible to look online to find others in a similar position. And it's worth doing, because it's still important to have contact with other mums in the same situation. You might find a working mums' group through Facebook. It's worth sniffing out other new mums at work – if your company is fairly big you might not realize, unless you look, that there are one or two other mums around. You can get together over lunch and share stories of juggling work and babycare. And the rest!

Making Friends

Once you find a group of mums, you need to get to know them. Obviously, you'll find it easier to connect with some mums than with others, but that's the same as any relationship. Just use the same principles that have shaped your friendships up to this point. For example, trust your gut feeling around others, talk to the people you feel drawn to and avoid those who make you feel uncomfortable or even anxious and insecure. Friendships should boost you and add something positive; they shouldn't drain you or leave you feeling lesser.

You won't necessarily click with every mother you meet, but the key to making new friends is to keep putting yourself out there.

Sometimes mums connect not through an organized group but just through mutual recognition, when they're in the same place at the same time. I know two mums who met in a coffee shop a couple of years ago. Both with a toddler in tow and a caffeine craving, they got talking and haven't looked back.

There are all sorts of other places where mums can meet –

playgrounds, doctors' waiting rooms, baby clinics, baby-relevant shops and so on. If you get chatting to someone you like, swap numbers and make the effort to call and arrange to meet again.

Once you do have some mum friends, aim to have regular time together without your children, if at all possible. While leaving the baby one night a week with your partner might make you feel guilty, it can be a lifesaver. A little bit of me-time with friends who understand the pleasures and pressures of motherhood is vital.

Friendship Challenges

Joining a new group of mothers isn't always easy, and neither is getting the balance right between being over-keen and too distant. Like any other kind of relationship, making friends with other mothers can throw up issues and challenges.

Choose Carefully

For a new mother, who is facing many changes and demands, both emotional and physical, there is the possibility of over-identification with or over-reliance on other mother friends. This will vary enormously between individuals and depend on their different circumstances. For example, if you have the misfortune to make friends with a mother who, for whatever reason, is overly critical, envious, selfish and self-centred, you might, understandably, lose confidence and internalize the situation, convincing yourself it's about some failing in you. So, it's important to choose potential new friends carefully, to develop the friendships over time and to maintain some boundaries around how much of your personal life you want to share and when. In other words, get to know new friends and don't just plunge in telling them absolutely everything. It can be overwhelming for you and for them.

The Playground Clique

The playground clique phenomenon is well known. At its worst, this can result in some mums forming such a tight group that newcomers or people who are in any way different are deliberately excluded. This is a big problem because not only are the mums unhappy and uncomfortable, on both the excluded and excluding sides of the fence, but they are providing an example of adult social behaviour to their children that no-one could possibly want to condone. If you happen to be the one whose face doesn't fit, then it is not a question of you changing but of finding others who have not given in to the group mindset. If the atmosphere is so toxic, then try talking to an approachable member of the school staff or someone on the governing body about ways of helping parents to get to know each other and hopefully be more positive in their relations.

How Do I Break In?

Sometimes the problem isn't the clique, it's the mum on the outside uncertain about how to join in. An established group can seem daunting and you can assume they are a clique who don't want you as a member. When that happens and you hold back, it can be you who appears standoffish, even though that's the last thing you feel. Or you may get the impression that they aren't the sort of group you want to join, for any number of reasons. But it's almost always worth giving it a go. Sometimes people aren't at all what we assume – a group that comes over as intimidating can turn out to be warm and friendly, once you get to know them as individuals.

The best way to break the ice is a simple smile and hello. You may be surprised to realize other mums are just as keen to make friends as you are.

Asking For Help

Sometimes we all need to ask for help. And most people are pleased to be asked and happy to offer help.

Whether the help you need is advice, an hour's childcare, or someone to cook you a meal because it's all feeling too much, don't hold back. Asking for help can be a great way of getting to know other mothers.

It might seem strange to suggest that asking for help is a skill, but it is. The ability to recognize when you need help, summon up the courage to ask for it, and follow through on that help is invaluable.

Diane says:

I feel quite strongly about how important a support network is in the life of a mother and I am so glad I had a group of friends around to share the ups and downs of early motherhood. We had a good group of friends BC (Before Children), so as babies came along the circle grew bigger and social activities shifted to involve children . . . fewer nights in the pub and more at friends' houses with babies in carry cots upstairs. I had a good friend who lived very close by and I would see her often. We'd go to mother and toddler groups together, where we would meet others and so the social circle got bigger. I would go round to other mums' houses for coffee etc. and the children would play while we chatted. It was invaluable for me, because my own mother was unable to help much due to illness (something that still saddens me now). Having friends around really helped with all the concerns and questions about early motherhood. We helped one another out, passed things on and shared our stories.

I am glad there are still plenty of mother and baby or toddler groups around in our area, as I believe mothers need to meet others and share experiences. I know we would always end up talking about babies/children/colic/weaning/potty training but it's a fantastic outlet and has probably saved many a marriage.

Everything changes when the dreaded world of work made a reappearance. At that point, there was a shift in the order of things and childcare became an issue. Which nursery school or child-minder should we use? We all entered the next stage of our lives. Friendships changed; my best friend moved away as her husband changed jobs. Some mothers went back to work full time and dropped off the social calendar as time with family became so precious. New people moved into the area and different friendships were made.

I decided not to go back to full-time teaching but to do supply work as it meant I would only need childcare a few days a month. I arranged to swap childcare with another teacher friend who also worked as a supply teacher and it worked well. We just made sure that we were never working on the same day.

Then the children started school and I met another group of mums. After chatting to a mum at the school bus stop I started to look after her two children for an hour after school every day. It fitted in with my hours, the children knew each other and it worked well.

Katie was a very sociable child, so she was often invited to have tea with school friends and in that way I met more mums so the support network continued. Of course, my husband David was the best support I had, but we did have times when we needed to call on friends to help out. When I went into labour with Suzy, my friend came over in the middle of the night and stayed with Paul and Katie and got them off to school the next morning. Another friend helped out when we had to go to London when my mum passed away.

We live in a fairly small town, which probably made it easier to make friends. But even in bigger towns and cities, I know there are strong networks of mothers, helping one another out and sharing the pleasures and the pains of motherhood. Without these networks I would worry that any new mother might suffer problems as a result of isolation.

I am very lucky that some of the mums I met through my children are still my friends today. It's something I would wish for any mother.

CHAPTER 5

Body Image

We are bombarded, online, on TV, on advertising hoardings and in magazines, by countless images of thin, happy-looking girls and women. And to impressionable young girls, they convey the idea that if you are really thin, preferably with well-developed breasts and long glossy hair, your world will be perfect.

All of this is leading to a huge rise in self-consciousness about looks in girls. And it's starting younger and younger. Three-year-olds, in one study, picked out a thin person and associated positive characteristics with that body shape. Six-year-olds can feel 'ugly' or 'fat'. Many eight-year-olds worry about what's in their lunchbox or whether they 'look right', and among older girls there's a dramatic rise in depression, self-harming and eating disorders, much of it associated with negative body image.

By the time girls become teenagers, they've had countless messages of what a female body 'should' look like. Physical beauty is increasingly expected to fit just one rule, and the current rule for beauty in the Western world is low body-weight combined with accentuated breast development. Something that is impossible for most girls to achieve.

Adults know that the images girls are fed are digitally enhanced and airbrushed. And adults know that, while the girls and women in the pictures are being paid to look happy, lots of them are actually unhappy. A lot of the people who are rewarded with modelling contracts and high fees for looking 'right' have deep emotional and psychological issues, eating disorders, health problems and a lack of confidence. The problem is that young girls don't know that these images are so often faked and they don't know what lies behind them.

It doesn't help that so many girls' clothes today are figure-hugging, midriff-baring styles. Or that mothers too often openly obsess about their own weight, or that dads and older brothers often make clear their preference for thinner women.

And then there's peer pressure. Girls post endless images of themselves online and 'like' or comment or message one another in response. Negative, critical and unkind comments are often among these responses. They're not the only responses, but they're the ones that girls tend to remember.

This is a subject that really worries me. I don't want my girls to grow up feeling bad about the way they look. I want Belle and Penelope to see their looks as just one aspect of who they are and to feel happy with themselves in every aspect.

So what can we, as mums, do to help? How can we encourage our daughters to feel good about the way they look? It seems like a tall order, especially when we're trying to bat against the power of the internet and the average three hours a day that girls spend online. But actually, there is a lot that we can do.

Self-Image

We all have an internal or mental picture of ourselves and we put this together in several ways. There are our measurable character-istics – like weight, hair and eye colour, skin tone and so on. And then there is what we choose to believe about ourselves from the way others behave towards us and the things they say.

Physical appearance has always been important in attracting friends and partners. But today it is more important than it has been at any other time in history. And this emphasis on physical looks is distorting the lives of countless young girls and many older women too.

During puberty, adolescents have the huge task of coping with major physical change and finding their own unique identities. If they are told often enough that they don't measure up to stand-ards of acceptability, by peers and adults in their own lives and in society at large, they can be especially vulnerable to seeing themselves negatively and to the related eating disorders, such as anorexia nervosa and bulimia, that can follow.

In response to these pressures, girls aren't just attempting to be thin. They are also getting fat. The incidence of obesity is increasing in the child, teenage and young adult population and, although many factors are involved, most research in this area links it with issues of poor body image. In other words, girls who feel bad about the way they look can be prone to over-eat as well as to under-eat.

From an increasingly young age, many girls struggle, in numerous ways, to conform to the 'gold standard' size zero image and the impossibility of achieving this makes them miserable and ill.

The focus on appearance in our image-obsessed culture is having a seriously worrying knock-on effect on all other aspects of girls' lives too. Girls are choosing to withdraw from activities because they feel they don't look good. The evidence is piling up that shows girls avoiding classroom discussion and debate, missing exams, skipping school and refusing to join in sports because of the way they think they look. It's a heartbreaking picture.

Young girls who should be doing well in school and sports, enjoying their friends and flourishing, are withdrawing from life because of the power of negative body image.

My Body Image

This is obviously an important area for me and one I will always be open and honest about with Belle and Penelope. They will know that mummy looks different and I will tell them why, bit by bit as they become old enough to understand. And I'll tell them how I feel about body image now and how I felt in the past.

As a young girl, I felt largely happy with my looks. I was a normal healthy weight, blonde and felt attractive , and although I didn't think I was perfect – far from it – I wasn't looks obsessed. But then I grew up in a pre-internet era. It sounds strange to say that – I think most of us feel the internet has always been a part of our lives. But just twenty years ago, when I was in my early teens, we didn't have smartphones and the internet. I got my first mobile at the age of fourteen and it was a clunky thing that only allowed me to text or call my friends. There was no Facebook, Snapchat, Instagram or Twitter. And because of that I was lucky. My friends and I loved clothes and doing our hair and make-up, but there were no cruel comments from strangers keeping us awake at night and any snippy remarks or petty conflicts were soon sorted out between us.

When I left school, I began training as a beautician and I loved it. But then I moved to London and set out to be a model and TV presenter. It was small scale, I got the occasional job for a cable company, I appeared at car shows and in catalogues and so on. And I had a lot of fun.

At that stage, the way I looked was important as part of my earning potential, so I did take a lot of trouble over my skin, hair and nails. But I also partied, had a good time, enjoyed life with my flatmates and worked hard to support myself.

Then, when I was twenty-four, my life changed in a moment. A man I had dated briefly paid another man who had never met me, to wait outside my flat with a cup of neat sulphuric acid, until I came out. And he threw it in my face.

The story of what happened next is well documented (and I will come back to it in the chapter on trauma). I was badly injured and I spent weeks in hospital and then months having surgery and starting a very long, hard road back to having any kind of life.

As a result of what happened, I lost everything – my home, my work and, of course, my looks. The acid burned my face, eye, ear, neck, chest and arm. And, as I swallowed some of it, it damaged me internally too; it was a long time before I could eat normally.

With the help of amazing medical staff who carried out numerous skin grafts, my face was gradually reconstructed. But it could never be the same. The face I have now is different to the face I once had. I have scars and I have had to come to terms with looking different, and with the looks and questions and comments that come my way.

What happened to me was awful. But it taught me something incredibly valuable; even though my body may be damaged and everything may be stripped away from me, I am still me. My spirit, the essence of me, remained intact. No-one can take away my will to live, my determination and my self-belief. What happened took me right back to the core of me and I discovered that I was strong and that I wanted to fight back, not just to live, but to live a rich, full life, to push boundaries and test myself to the limit. I wasn't going to let the men who hurt me win. So I wear my scars with pride, I don't hide away or apologize, I appear on TV as a presenter, I give talks, I run my charity and I appear at all kinds of public functions. I love dressing up, I love glamorous shoes and having my hair done and being feminine. Why should I let all that go, or feel ashamed, or stay out of sight because two wicked people hurt me?

These are the things I hope to teach my daughters. To be proud of who they are, to accept differences and to know that, if their spirit is strong, they can withstand anything.

I get trolling and nasty comments online. But I get far more encouraging, positive and appreciative comments. I've learned to ignore the trolls, or to feel sorry for them, and to be grateful for all the goodness and kindness, humour and appreciation that comes my way.

Belle is growing up fast now and I have already begun to tell her about what happened to me and why mummy looks different. I talk to her in a very straightforward way, giving her only the information she asks for, a little at a time. And as small children do, she accepts it all as perfectly normal, nods and then runs off to play. When the time comes, I will tell Penelope in the same way. I hope that dealing with their mum's experiences – and no doubt having to answer questions from school friends in the future – will help both girls to become accepting of all kinds of differences, and compassionate and tolerant towards others. And I hope that this acceptance will extend to themselves, and that they will always think of their own bodies as normal, loveable and a source of pride.

The Influence of Mothers

When it comes to a girl's self-image there is no more important influence than her mother.

Girls take to heart what their mothers say about bodies: their own, their daughters, those of strangers and celebrities.

If a mother is constantly critical, or if she places a lot of emphasis on her daughter's looks and shows little interest in her other characteristics and abilities, then her daughter can spend her whole life dealing with feelings of not being good enough.

More important even than what a mother says is what she does. A mother who is picky about what she eats and is constantly on diets or 'watching her weight' will set this up as a way of eating for her daughter. A mother who talks about being fat or drops casual remarks like 'that's going straight to my hips' will make her daughter as body-conscious as she is. A mother who criticises her body and says things like 'I look huge in that' or 'look at that tummy, I have to do something about it' will give her daughter the impression that self-criticism is the norm.

The mother may well be repeating her own experience of being treated harshly, but while an adult can see her judgement is skewed, a child – even a teenager – just doesn't have enough life experience and the emotional and cognitive resources to take this into account. She will take it very literally and accept that her mother is right. These negative feelings are known as self-attributions. And they can be hard to shift, even when the child has become an adult and learned to be more aware of what others say and do, and of their motives.

What Mothers Can Do

To change what is often a pattern of self-criticism and misery passed down through generations, mothers need to emphasize health, wellbeing and happiness unconnected with looks.

You can't hide every magazine, turn off every TV or take away phones and computers. Banning any of these will just single your daughter out from her friends, who will all have the same devices, magazines and toys. And that will make her miserable. You can, of course, limit time spent on any device. Phones in the bedroom at night, for instance, aren't a good idea for all sorts of reasons. But that won't solve the problem.

Experts suggest that parents' energy is better spent getting their daughters to look at and think critically about the unrealistic way the media portrays girls and women. The key is for parents to watch or play with or look at whatever their daughters are alongside them. That way you can say things like, 'Wow, nobody I've ever known is really that thin,' or 'What do you think about girls who are so thin?'

If your daughter is old enough, mention that if you're very thin your periods will stop and you may have other health problems. Talk about eating disorders and the fact that a lot of thin girls in the public eye suffer from them. I'm not suggesting you bombard your daughter with facts; it needs to be a relaxed conversation, or many conversations, where your daughter gives her thoughts and views too.

Tell her about airbrushing and how it can make someone look thinner, or hide blemishes. Play with photoshopping on the computer, digitally altering and manipulating images, so that she can see how easy it is to make someone look a certain way. Point out that no real women look so 'perfect'. If you encourage your daughter to think about the images of woman she sees and to begin to make judgements for herself, then you've made a vital step forwards.

Introduce her to different ideas of beauty. Voluptuous women, women of different sizes, with different kinds of faces and hair and skin tones. Comment positively on women you see who are unusual or different. Lead your daughter gently away from the narrow 'idealized' images that girls are so often fed and open her eyes to the real world and all its infinite varieties of beauty.

Talk to your daughter about what it means to be healthy too. Being fit, active, full of energy and focused on the activities in your day, not your looks, is healthy.

Ways to support your daughter's positive body image:

- Draw attention to beautiful women and men who do not conform to society's ideals.
- Try to make your comments about your own and other women's appearances constructive and fair.
- Initiate conversations about how to be healthy and fit.
- Make sure you acknowledge and value not only your daughter's appearance but her other attributes and achievements.
- Accept your own imperfections, whatever you judge them to be, and it'll be second nature for your daughter to do the same.
- Get active and provide a good model of physical exercise plus balanced and healthy eating.
- Appreciate and enjoy your daughter's journey from girl to woman.
- Show interest in her – what does she love to do, what does she think, who are her friends?

EXERCISE:
A LETTER TO YOUR
YOUNGER SELF

Try writing a letter to your younger self, telling her the things you have learned about growing up from a girl into a woman. Start by acknowledging and appreciating all the things your unique body has allowed you to do and all the fun you've had, not least having a child or children. Remember the doubts and worries that you had as a girl and when puberty started, and advise your own child self from the position of hindsight. What you learn from this exercise is worth bearing in mind for the conversations you have with your own daughter.

A Word About Dads

Fathers play a hugely influential role in shaping their daughters' self-image. While girls model themselves on their mothers, they learn how to relate to men from their fathers.

Girls need to feel that their fathers love, appreciate and respect them. If a girl has a strong and secure relationship with her father, then she has a good chance of finding that for herself in her adult life.

Comedian and writer Dawn French remembers her father sitting her down as a teenager and telling her how beautiful and precious she was. In that way, she says, her dad 'armed her for life'. 'He wanted to make sure that, because I was a bigger girl, I didn't ever think less of myself, or that I didn't deserve the best.'

In addition to telling their daughters that they are beautiful, dads can make their daughters feel good about themselves, and their bodies, in other ways:

Spend time with them – just father and daughter on their own, every now and then. If there is more than one daughter, they each need separate time with Dad.

Point out what it is about them that makes them special or unique. 'You really know a lot about . . .' or 'You're getting so good at playing the guitar . . .' or 'You are the best tree-climber I know.' Or any one of a hundred things that is not about their looks and that will make them glow with pride and give them confidence.

Ask their opinion – 'What do you think about x or y?' Show real interest.

Listen to them. Dads tend to problem-solve. Sometimes just listening is better. Especially when they are feeling unhappy.

Be a man who respects all women, who treats them equally, never makes sexist comments or jokes, and who comments only on the qualities and abilities women have – e.g., 'She's a great politician.'

Talk to her about sex. Mums need to do this too, but fathers can emphasize the importance of making choices, never letting boys pressure you, taking your time getting to know someone, staying safe and how precious your body is.

When Problems Begin

It's important to keep a close eye out for any escalating problems that your daughter might be developing. Look out for signs of secrecy, of poor health, of unusual behaviour around mealtimes and of changes in routine, friendships or activities.

Teenagers who have a very poor self-image are vulnerable to a number of conditions. These include extreme anxiety, eating disorders such as anorexia and bulimia, and a condition that is now on the increase called body dysmorphic disorder (BDD). This is an anxiety disorder, and sufferers – they can be girls or boys but the majority are girls – develop extremely negative and unrealistic views about their appearance. They can also develop compulsive behaviours and routines as a way of coping with negative and obsessional thoughts. If left untreated, depression, anxiety and eating disorders can develop.

A girl with BDD may obsess about her weight, her features or one particular feature – her nose, for instance, or her lips, or forehead. She will begin to feel so self-conscious that it affects her behaviour, her health and her wellbeing.

Possible signs of BDD include:

Frequently checking in the mirror

Talking about herself, or an aspect of her looks, as ugly or not right

Getting distressed about the features she feels are ugly

Avoiding one or more activities, like parties, after-school activities, dance classes

Being preoccupied with looks a lot of the time

Thinking everyone is looking at her when she is out of the home

Asking whether surgery is possible for the perceived flaw(s)

Starting to use heavy make-up

Obsessively weighing herself, or exercising

If you think your child is suffering from BDD or any other disorder as a result of her poor body image, then contact your GP. Insist the situation is taken seriously and that she is given support and help in the form of counselling.

Ginny and Chloe's Story

Mum Ginny tells the story:

Chloe's problems seemed to appear soon after she started secondary school. At eleven, she was a little chubby – not fat, just with a little bit of puppy fat that had appeared in the previous year and that made her face more rounded. Her figure was still that of a little girl, she hadn't yet developed curves.

She hadn't been self-conscious at all before that. We talked about the puppy fat and I told her that it was normal, I'd had the same thing, and it would drop off in the next year or two. I made sure our meals were well balanced and she wasn't over-eating, so I didn't worry. Until she got to her new school and some of the other children began bullying her.

Within a few months, Chloe had changed so much. She had always been chatty and outgoing but she became withdrawn and began combing her hair so that it almost covered her face. She started weighing herself a lot and refusing meals and when I asked her what was going on she burst into tears and said, 'I'm so ugly.'

It broke my heart. Chloe was a perfectly normal, nice-looking girl. But when she broke down she told me that a small group of cruel girls at school were taunting her all the time, telling her she was fat and ugly, and asking her how she could bear even looking in the mirror.

I was so shaken when I realized how unhappy she was that I went to our GP to ask what help there might be. The GP was sympathetic and referred us to a local eating disorders clinic. Chloe didn't yet have a specific eating disorder, but she did have the beginnings of body dysmorphic disorder. We saw a really good counsellor at the clinic, who talked to us together and then started seeing Chloe once a week.

I also went to see the headteacher at school. She was very good too. She held an assembly on bullying, and the subject of looks, and self-confidence was brought into the PSHE (personal, social, health and economic) lessons. And the girls who had been bullying Chloe were asked in to see the head, who talked to them about the damage they were doing.

All these things made a difference. Chloe saw the counsellor for six months and at school things got a lot better for her. One of the girls who had been bullying her became a friend and encouraged her into a group of girls where she gradually began to feel more confident.

Two years on Chloe was a happier, healthier girl. I still kept a close eye on her, but I felt we'd had a close shave and it could have been far worse.

A Healthy Attitude to Food

Many teenage girls begin to eat in a picky way – avoiding some foods and sometimes obsessing about others. They may worry about becoming too fat and think they should avoid certain foods, but few have any idea of what a healthy balanced diet is or the harm that can be done by cutting out certain foods from their diet. And it's not just teenagers – a recent study found that up to 60 percent of six- to twelve-year-olds worry about their weight and the way they look.

There's a lot mums can do to avoid this, or nip it in the bud if it's beginning. At home, the aim should be for the family to eat together as often as possible; a balanced meal in which everyone eats the same foods and the focus is on conversation, not the meal. And for packed lunches, aim to prepare them together with your daughter, discussing what will give her a healthy but filling and balanced meal. Talk to her about what food does for our bodies and how poorly we can function without proper nutrition, including all the major food groups.

Here are some strategies that work well in keeping your daughter's eating on track.

Have 'Sometimes' and 'Always' Foods

Avoid categorizing any foods as good or bad. Instead talk about 'sometimes' foods and 'always' foods. This way you don't ban any food, you just make it easy to remember which foods we need and should have daily, and which foods are better eaten in small quantities, less often.

Banning something – we all know this – just makes us want it more. So don't have anything off limits, just aim for moderation. In the past (I'm talking about when I was a child), there was so much less focus on food. We had our meals, had a few treats and that was it. Of course, there were people with eating issues and disorders. But the numbers were so much lower, and there wasn't the current obsession with 'superfoods' and which food is great or terrible. So, make vegetables, fruits, whole grains, proteins and dairy products the 'always' foods that are useful and necessary for growth and development. And sweets and fried foods can be seen as 'sometimes' foods that taste good but are not healthy or necessary to help us grow.

Help Her to Know When She's Had Enough

Encourage your child, from the start, to know when she feels full. If a child isn't particularly hungry at a mealtime, don't make her eat everything on her plate. Talk to her about eating only when hungry and how to stop when full. Ask her about when her stomach feels growly and empty, and when it feels heavy and full.

This 'self-attuned eating' can be the best way to avoid future eating disorders. It helps children to feel safe and comfortable around food. There are no pressures to eat certain foods, or a certain amount. They can learn to recognize when they feel satisfied and to stop eating. Allowing children to decide when, what and how much to eat helps to strengthen their self-confidence and self-esteem, and give them a sense of dignity.

Involve Her in the Process

Get your child involved in choosing and preparing foods –
meals at home and packed lunches if she has them. Take her
shopping and choose foods together, talking about what it
would be nice to have. Steer her towards food in the 'always'
groups, but pick a few fun 'sometimes' foods too. The idea is
that food, the preparation and the eating, can be fun and that
we all have choices and can choose foods that help us to be
strong and healthy. Talk about certain foods, for instance 'we
eat carrots because they have vitamins and they're good for
our eyesight'. Choose recipes together and teach her to cook.
Most children who enjoy food, know about nutrition and are
involved in cooking, don't develop eating disorders and body-
image problems.

Physical Activity

The benefits of being physically active are enormous, for all of
us. Healthier bodies and brains dramatically reduce the likelihood of anxiety or depression. Exercise can blow away a bad
mood and teenagers who are physically active tend to have a
healthier body image. They see their body as something to be
proud of, for what it can achieve, and something to take care
of. So making sure that your daughter is physically active right
from the start is vital. You're giving her an essential life skill
she can always rely on.

It's worth putting some thought into which activities you
encourage. There are some which encourage girls to focus on

93

their looks, which encourage perfectionism and have become more sexualized. Most girls in the UK take dance classes at some point; it's a part of childhood for many of us. So I'm not suggesting that you don't take your child to dance classes. But be alert to the possibility that there can be problems further down the line. The same goes for gymnastics and ice skating.

Research shows that girls who participate in sports that don't emphasize leanness are likely to feel better about themselves. It's a way of defining themselves that is not about appearance.

Experiment with different kinds of sports, because every girl will be different. But don't accept no sport, just because she isn't naturally athletic. Not everyone can be in the first team, but everyone can get a buzz out of moving their body and recognizing that having some stamina and some muscle makes you feel good and look good too. So don't let it be optional – just as she has to help around the house or do her homework, she needs to take exercise.

Set the example yourself. If she sees you going to the gym, or for a run, or to play tennis, then that becomes the norm.

Towards a Healthy Body Image

As mums, we want our daughters to feel good about their bodies, throughout their lives. And there's so much we can do to encourage this. Making sure they exercise and eat well is the foundation stone for a lifelong healthy body image. And the surest way to do this is to set the example ourselves. I love to go running and to feel strong and fit, and I hope my girls will see from my example that daily exercise is just a part of life. I also enjoy my food. I love fruit and veg, but I also like tucking into a roast dinner (Richie's speciality) or a plate of shepherd's pie.

There are a couple of other things that I think help girls to see their bodies positively. One of these is being careful about the way they dress. Shops now are full to the brim with pro-vocative clothing for young girls, and when parents allow their young daughters to dress like this it sends sexual messages that neither the parents nor the girls intend – and it can lead to girls finding themselves in sexual situations they are just not ready for. Sexy clothing at school is never a good idea, and outside school it needs to be carefully monitored. Apart from anything else, a girl who gets a lot of attention for being 'hot' may start to think that she's not valued for anything else, and stop bothering with her schoolwork.

I believe in women enjoying their sexuality. But until the second half of their teens, girls aren't ready and they need to be focused on other things.

The other thing that helps is to encourage your daughter to accept any 'flaws' that she perceives in her body. You can be sympathetic, but also confident that whatever she doesn't like about herself is not the end of the world. You want her to include both these attitudes in her self-talk, so that she might think, 'This is tough,' and at the same time, 'I'm strong and I can cope with it.'

Promoting a healthy body image means helping your daughter feel beautiful overall – the whole person that she is – and at the same time taking the emphasis off beauty and sexuality as the focus of her identity. Girls who have confidence, who are sure of themselves as *people*, not as sexual objects, are not only likely to wait longer to have sex, but are more able to hold their own in today's high-pressure world.

CHAPTER 6

Friendships

Friendships are such an important part of life. Friends are the people we laugh with, share with and can rely on when times get tough.

That's why we want our children to be able to make friends, to feel confident in new situations, to be part of a friendship group and to have enduring friendships that last through childhood and into adult life. But friendships aren't without their pitfalls, so we also want our children to be able to choose wisely, not to follow a troublemaker blindly and to know who is and is not a real friend and when to let a 'friendship' go.

Some children make friends easily; others are shy and need encouragement. So how do you help them navigate the world of friendships so that they feel confident and happy with the friends they have around them? And what happens when, inevitably, there's conflict and hurt and your child realizes a friend isn't always on their side?

In an ideal world you love your children's friends, but what do you do when your child has a new friend you instinctively don't like? Can you keep your child away from someone you feel is a bad influence? And what if it is your child another mum thinks is the one leading their child astray?

Then there's the 'friendship' world of social media, which is so much a part of children's lives from an increasingly early age. How soon do you let them have a mobile phone? Go on Facebook? Have a Snapchat or Instagram account? How do you monitor what they're up to and how do you help a child who is being bullied online, or one who is far too open with strangers? How do you teach a child who thinks that everyone is a friend to keep themselves safe while enjoying the world of social media, and to understand the perils of online grooming?

All these questions and many more concern me as I watch my daughters start stepping into the world of other children and friendships. And I know I'm not alone – every mum I talk to has the same questions and worries.

The Importance of Friendships

Human beings are social creatures and we live in a social world. For children, their first social experiences are largely with adults but the adult–child relationship is not the equal one that is necessary for friendship. The parenting role requires the adult to be protector, provider, carer and instructor, and this sets the rules of the relationship. The relationship between children, however, is on a more level playing field as they have to negotiate with each other, learn to give and take, and in so doing operate in a similar way to adults in the grown-up world. When the child is with other children, they cannot necessarily have things exactly the way they would like them, they have to compromise and learn to modify their demands and behaviours in order to build friendships; for example, learning to take turns, sharing and dealing with others' needs.

Very young, pre-school-aged children tend to be all about 'me'. They haven't yet learned how to build friendships, they want to play and, while they do sometimes play together, they haven't yet learned to negotiate, and playtime sometimes ends in tears.

A child has to learn to gradually become less self-focused in her early social interactions with other children and in doing this she begins to mature in a number of very important areas:

- She develops a unique identity and sense of belonging.
- She builds the understanding, knowledge and skills to live harmoniously with other people.
- She develops language and communication skills.
- Her emotional awareness increases.

All of these are necessary building blocks in a child's personal foundations for learning of every kind and in becoming an effective and independent person as an adult. So friendship is not just a lovely thing – it's a vital stepping stone to growing up as a fully functioning human being.

Having said that, developing friendship skills takes time. It's a long, slow process and it happens most effectively for those children with involved parents who communicate well with them.

It's worth mentioning here the differences between genders. For the vast majority of children, there will be differences in the ways that girls and boys play together and form friendships. Children learn very young about the ways in which girls and boys behave and that these are not always the same. Both girls and boys tend to stick largely to same-gender friends and to play in different ways. Most parents will notice that boys often play noisily, with plenty of yelling, whooping, play-fighting and running around the house. While girls often play more quietly and tend to gravitate to games that are more static and often involve discussion and transaction.

Recent research indicates that these differences are not created by society – girls and boys are born with their preferences. One theory is that boys are drawn to anything involving movement and activity – possibly a result of early man's need to hunt and gather. And girls' tendency to play in a more cooperative and mutually supportive way is possibly a result of early woman's need to nurture children and keep them safe.

I Loved Friends

I was one of those incredibly sociable children. I would go up to other children and say, 'I'm Katie, can I play with you?' I started playgroup when I was three and I loved it, and it was the same when I got to primary school – I had lots of friends and talked my head off non-stop – in and out of class. One of my school reports said, 'If Katie would only stop talking, she could do very well.' That was me summed up!

When I went to secondary school I had a bit of a blip. My two best friends went to a different school and I had to start again, aged eleven, knowing no-one. I was upset about it and at first I felt I hated the school, but that didn't last for long, I soon got stuck in and made new friends.

As a teenager, I tended to be one of the ringleaders in my group of friends. And I was always pushing the boundaries. I would be hitching up my skirt, chopping the end off my tie, getting caught smoking and arguing with my parents about going out. I lost count of the times I was grounded.

Friends were a huge part of my world growing up and of course I want that to be the same for Belle and Penelope. Belle is already very like I was – a proper little show-off, always singing, dancing and wanting to play with anyone and everyone. So I hope she won't have problems making friends, and I hope I'll be able to help her navigate through the ups and downs of friendship. Penelope is still too young for us to know whether she's another 'everyone's a friend' girl, or perhaps a bit more quiet and thoughtful in her approach. I can't wait to see. We'll certainly do our best to encourage her to make friends, because making friends is one of the most important things in life.

Encouraging Your Child to Make Friends

Like every other skill your child acquires, learning to make friends takes time. And like everything else, it isn't a straight line from A to Z, it's an up and down process, in which there are times when they seem to take a step backwards. In other words, they may appear to have grasped something, such as making new friends, and then the next moment they'll have a setback and have to rebuild this particular skill.

You may think that making friends is just something you do and that it doesn't take skill at all. But, actually, it takes all kinds of skills and it certainly doesn't come naturally to everyone. Making friends means learning social skills, and these include having a two-way conversation, sharing, learning about give and take, and discovering how to deal with conflict and upset. This might start when two toddlers want the same toy and it all ends in tears. The way you deal with this can be the difference between your child moving forwards with the friendship, or taking a step back.

The children who develop good friendship skills generally have positive involved parents and extended family, who are supportive and communicate well with them and who provide healthy role models of how to make, keep, enjoy and manage friendships.

Children will discover friendships at different ages. Some children are perfectly happy playing with their siblings and cousins, and there isn't any real problem. All their needs for companionship are being met at home, so they won't seek out friends until they feel the need to. These children usually make friends once they decide that it is important to them, because they've been learning social skills within their family.

Then there are the children who would like to make friends, but don't really know how. They might be shy, or they might not understand the 'rules' of social interaction. Or they might have an early experience – perhaps another child becoming very angry – which makes them nervous or afraid.

The tips below cover some of the areas to be aware of, but only you know your child and what will work best with them. Often when a child is shy or uncertain and perhaps finding playgroup overwhelming, the best way forward is to arrange to have just one child over to play. Friendships start one to one, and once your child has one friend they will find it easier to make others. When they make this first connection, they can then translate that into a group situation and it will become easier for them.

Top tips for supporting your child in developing friendship skills:

- Provide opportunities at home and outside of school that allow children to be with other children the same age and to engage in a variety of activities and shared interests, with parents on hand to deal with any falling out and to ensure play is safe and appropriate.
- Join the child in their play with make-believe friends when they are very small and talk with them about friendship.
- Watch films and television programmes that are about friendships, talk to them about these and be available to answer their questions.
- Choose books that feature stories about friendship and read these together. Again, talking and answering questions about the stories is important. You know the level of your child's understanding and their particular interests

103

so use this knowledge to find books you think they will like. (The same goes for films and television programmes.)

- Make sure that you, as adults, provide examples of the joys of friendship through keeping up with your own friends and integrating contact with them into family life. It's obviously easier to do this with friends who also have children of similar ages to your own but this doesn't mean that childless friends have to be dropped as there may well be benefits to adults and children alike from continuing to socialize with them. And of course, the friendship has its own value.

Sue and Belinda's Story

Belinda had a difficult start in life. Her birth was long and complicated, and after over twenty-four hours in labour her mother Sue required an emergency caesarean. Belinda then spent over a week in the special baby care unit because of breathing difficulties. After this, her early months were relatively problem-free, but Sue was a worrier and was incredibly protective of Belinda. She would never take up babysitting offers from her family or friends and devoted every waking minute to her daughter's care. She refused to allow Belinda to attend a playgroup or nursery and would only let other children play with her daughter if she could be present and supervise the play to the point that she never let the children just play together on their own.

When Belinda turned five, starting school was drawn-out and distressing. Sue, still reluctant to leave her child, managed to persuade the nursery staff to allow her to stay in class with Belinda but it soon became apparent that the little girl would never properly connect with the other children until her mother stepped back and learnt to trust the school with her daughter's safety.

The educational psychologist for the school was asked to help. She could see that Sue and Belinda had reached the point where neither felt they could manage without the other; a situation that wasn't good for either of them. After meeting with the school staff, the psychologist set up a plan to help Sue and Belinda to separate during school hours, so that Belinda could start making healthy relationships with others.

It took most of the first term to do this, in small steps, encouraging Sue to leave Belinda first for a couple of hours, and then for a bit longer. Eventually Sue settled into the same routine as the other parents, dropping off Belinda in the mornings and returning to collect her in the afternoons.

At this stage Belinda's life at school was transformed. She gradually became less shy and clingy with the staff and began to play with the other children. By the end of the year she had developed several early friendships with boys and girls in her class and she persuaded her mum to let her have occasional play dates at her home. It took longer for Sue to allow Belinda to go to other children's homes but, in time, this happened too.

When Friendships Go Wrong

It's always hard when your child is hurt or upset by a friend. Your first instinct is to protect your child, perhaps by ticking off the other child or by removing your child from the scene. But if the situation is not putting either child in danger, it's worth holding fire and encouraging your child to sort the difficulty out for themselves.

Remember also that you don't have a lot of influence over other children (or their parents). You have much more influence over helping your own child to develop good skills for coping with the situation.

Just as girls and boys tend to play differently, their conflicts (and ways of bullying one another) are often different too. Boys, traditionally, are more likely to engage in physical acts of aggression and intimidation, whereas girls can engage in psychological or emotional acts of aggression and aversion, such as excluding a girl from a friendship group or making personal comments about her appearance, clothes or family.

It's useful to be aware of these patterns, but it's still important to clarify exactly what happened, who was affected, how they are feeling and to work towards a resolution, because every conflict situation is unique. Teachers are in a great position to model and educate their pupils in handling conflict through the personal, social, health and economic (PSHE) curriculum and also because they can, to a great extent, supervise and control the social context in the school environment. Parents have an equally important role to play outside school and they too can model respect for differences and effective, positive ways not only of handling differences but also of welcoming them.

Encouraging your child to resolve things themselves, with supervision from you if they are very small, or with support and discussion from you if the problem is at school or the child is older than five or six, empowers the child and helps them to feel that they can manage difficult situations in life. If they need to rely on you to fight their battles, they will not develop self-belief and confidence.

This encouragement doesn't mean just saying, 'Sort it out yourself.' What you can say is things like:

- What do you think the problem is?
- What have you tried so far?
- What could you try now that might work?

You can 'brainstorm' ideas with your child, writing down every possibility you can both think of before choosing one. And you can role-play too, it's a great way of allowing your child to practise what they want to say or do, while you play the other child.

Communication

The poet William Blake wrote these words over 200 years ago:

I was angry with my friend:
I told my wrath, my wrath did end.
I was angry with my foe:
I told it not, my wrath did grow.
(A Poison Tree)

His words capture many truths about the thorny subject of dealing with conflict but, essentially, the most important point is that conflict can only truly be resolved with good communication.

The more your child is able to speak for themselves, to discuss, negotiate and – vitally – to listen, the better they will be at resolving conflict. If she can tell the other child why she is upset, listen to what the other child has to say and come up with a resolution, she has skills that will be invaluable throughout her life.

EXERCISE:
CONFLICT RESOLUTION

Psychologist Kairen Cullen passed on the following exercise, which is useful for helping children to own, understand and express their difficulties.

After a difficult incident, take a sheet of paper and a pen or pencil and divide the page into three sections. In the first section, write 'FACTS', the second 'FEELINGS' and the third 'WISHES'. Actually, this is a winning formula for children and adults alike. If you can sort out in your own mind what actually happened, how you feel and what you want to happen, and then communicate this effectively, there is every chance you can find a resolution.

THE RESOLUTION SHEET	
Name: Date:	
FACTS What happened?	
FEELINGS How did you feel?	
WISHES What do you want to happen now?	
	Write in one sentence what you can do now:

A friend of mine, Julia, did this with her ten-year-old daughter Stacey, after Stacey came home from school very upset because she and her friend Caitlyn had quarrelled.

Children often only give us part of the story; most often the part that casts themselves in the role of the helpless victim. So Julia, while concerned and sympathetic, did not jump to blame Caitlyn. Instead, she drew up the resolution sheet and when Stacey had calmed down, an hour or so after coming home, she suggested they fill it in together.

'What happened?' Julia asked.

Stacey explained, after some hesitation, that she and Caitlyn both wanted the same part in the school play. Caitlyn had been given the role and was 'being a show-off about it'. Stacey, her pride wounded, had told Caitlyn she was 'no good at acting and would be rubbish in the play'. Caitlyn had stormed off, saying she wouldn't speak to Stacey any more.

'So how did this argument make you feel?' Julia asked.

Stacey said she felt angry, and hurt, and then sad. She didn't want to lose Caitlyn as a friend.

'What would you like to happen now?' Julia asked.

Stacey said she wanted to be friends with Caitlyn again. But she didn't want Caitlyn to go on and on about getting the part.

Julia talked to Stacey about why Caitlyn might have been 'going on' about it – that she probably felt excited and proud of herself. And she explained that Caitlyn probably didn't realize how hurt Stacey was feeling about not getting the part.

'Do you think Caitlyn might be feeling hurt too, after what you said?' Julia asked. Stacey agreed, a little reluctantly, that she might.

'What could you do now?' Julia said.

Stacey thought for a minute. 'I guess I could say sorry and tell her she's my friend and it doesn't matter about the play,' she said.

And that's what she did. Caitlyn said sorry too, and Stacey got a different part in the play, so both girls were happy.

Most conflicts can be sorted out relatively easily and quickly. If this is not possible then you might need to enlist the help of other adults such as the child's teacher or possibly, if appropriate, the other parent. Be cautious about stepping in too quickly, though, as children can often sort it out themselves and in the worst-case scenario the parents become antagonistic with each other, siding, naturally enough, with their own children and then not communicating effectively and constructively with each other.

One of the best ways of sorting out a conflict is to organize a play-date for your child and the other child. Most children are nicer and find communicating with one another easier in a one-to-one setting. Friendships are more powerful than group dynamics, if those friendships are nurtured. If a play-date with the other child is not possible, then nurturing her other friendships in one-to-one situations is a good buffer against the nasty stuff that can happen in groups.

The Pre-teen Years

Girls have most friendship difficulties between the ages of eight and eleven. It can be a tricky time for their social development, partly because at this age they begin to be influenced by the broader social culture. Until now their parents have been the biggest influence. But from around year 4 in primary school the influence of other children, and of the media, starts to come into play.

One research study showed that girls' self-esteem plummets after reading teen fashion or celebrity magazines. They can begin to feel they're not pretty or clever or good enough. And, given that women and girls only appear on screen, in films and on TV a third as much as men and boys, girls can also begin to feel that they aren't as important as boys.

All of this can set up an atmosphere of competition between girls that wasn't there when they were younger.

It's sad to think that the media, and social media, can have such a hugely negative impact on growing girls. Thankfully a lot is being done to identify and counteract this. Women, and men, are talking about it and doing more to change it. One great example is actress Geena Davis, who set up an organization called seejane.org, which aims to get women more representation on screen and to put right the gender bias in the media, giving girls a more positive message about themselves.

When Friendships End

Sadly, sometimes friendships do end. It's happened to all of us at one time or another and it's almost always upsetting. For a young girl who is suddenly 'dropped' by a friend, it can feel devastating.

Sometimes, it's not even possible to know why it has happened. It's often because the other girl has made a 'cooler' friend or joined a new crowd. But even if you do know why you're being ignored, it doesn't lessen the hurt.

If this happens to your daughter, all you can do is sympathize. It hurts, but it will pass. It's normal, in the sense that it happens to almost everyone at some time. And it seldom leaves an emotional scar, even though it feels at the time as though it will.

This is where your daughter gets the chance to build her resilience. Don't overdo the sympathy to the point where she sees herself as a victim, and do encourage her into other friendships along the lines of, 'You've always liked Megan, why don't you ask her to come over at the weekend?'

She may grieve the loss of this friend for a while, but that's only human. And, as with all things that you can't change, she simply has to face it and move on.

When You Don't Like Their Friends

This can be a tricky one. Your daughter brings home her 'amazing' new friend and you don't like her. It might be simply a feeling that this isn't the right kind of friend for your child, or it might be something that the child does, or says, or even a manner. All you know is, you'd rather your child wasn't friends with her, but your child thinks she's brilliant.

Here's a quick checklist of what to do:

- First, and most importantly, don't tell your daughter that you don't like her friend.
- Try to work out why you don't like the other child. Is it something she is doing? Or is it simply a feeling you have?
- Try getting to know the child better. Include her, talk to her and take an interest in her. Sometimes this really works – you and the child both relax, and any problems seem to dissolve.
- If that doesn't work or isn't possible, stay neutral. Don't encourage your daughter to see the other child, but don't forbid it either.
- Talk to your daughter, in a relaxed way, about why she likes the other child and what she gets out of the friendship. The insight from this may help you to accept the other child.

- If all else fails, wait patiently. It may well be that the friendship fizzles out as your daughter comes to realize that her friend is not right for her.

The situation is different if you think another child is a seriously bad influence on your child, for instance if she is encouraging your child to bully others, if she is encouraging her to try alcohol or drugs, or if your child has been doing badly at school since the friendship began.

It's always worth talking to your child's teacher to get a sense of whether it might be a damaging relationship or not. Teachers see so many children's friendships, they're in a good position to know when it's necessary to worry.

It's easier to actively discourage or end a friendship if your child is young – you can divert your child towards other friendships. When the child is approaching the teenage years, it gets harder. Forbidding a friendship could backfire, but talking to your child during a calm moment, rather than in the middle of a power struggle, can help the child open up about the friendship and what she gets from that connection. Keep the communication channels open and keep talking to your child, with respect and interest, rather than obvious disapproval. You might need to say things like, 'Friends don't make you feel unhappy, or put pressure on you.'

Bear in mind also that if your child is part of a group you think is bad news, your child might be a leader rather than someone swept up in things. Everyone thinks, 'Not my child,' but it's more helpful to think, 'Could it be my child?' And if it could be, approach the conversations from that perspective.

It's always useful to talk to, and work with, other parents if you can. Parents working together can make a real difference. So, if you feel there's a problem child, try to get their parents on side, rather than putting their backs up.

Tina and Emma's Story

Eight-year-olds Emma and Jade had been friends for a couple of years. Tina, Emma's mum, had always felt uneasy about it, as the friendship involved a lot of competition, jealousy and arguments that didn't happen in Emma's other friendships. However, Emma seemed to adore Jade, who not only went to the same school but lived a few doors away.

As time went by, Tina became more concerned about how bossy Jade was. She seemed to want to control Emma. She refused to let Emma make friends with other girls at school, she told Emma what she should wear and she insisted they play together every day.

Emma went along with all this, and seemed happy, but Tina worried that Emma wasn't getting as much out of school as she could and that she should have other friendships. She felt Jade was standing between Emma and everyone else.

Tina decided to have a word with the girls' teacher, Mrs Potter. She was helpful, and she agreed that the friendship was very intense and that it might be a good thing for both girls to make other friends as well.

Tina decided to have a chat with Jade's mum Sophie, who

she knew fairly well and liked. She approached the problem diplomatically, knowing that any hint of criticism might put up barriers. She suggested that, as the teacher had said, the friendship was a little intense and said she wondered whether the girls should limit their time together outside school, just to allow them room to make other friends. Sophie was surprised but she agreed, on the basis that it was in both girls' interest.

For the next couple of months, Emma and Jade only played together once a week – the mums told them they needed more time for homework and activities. While both girls objected to this, Emma soon accepted it. Tina encouraged her to ask other friends over, one to one, and Emma was soon good friends with two other girls. This spilled over into school, where Mrs Potter reported that Jade and Emma were no longer joined at the hip but were both part of a bigger circle. It was only some time later that Emma told Tina, 'I'm glad Jade stopped coming over so much, she was a bit bossy.'

Friendships and Social Media

Parents now have to help their children manage and deal with online 'virtual' friendships too. And this can be tough; sometimes the distinction between 'real' and 'virtual' friends gets lost – even for adults, never mind children. However, it is important to make this distinction. Real friends are people with whom you want to spend time. Virtual friends are those you spend time communicating with online. The two are very different and it's important that online activity does not substitute for those active, face-to-face shared times that are so key to a child's social and overall development.

Social media can be emotionally safer, less demanding and much easier to control. But it is not in children's best interests to overdo the social media activities, and keeping them safe from online predators and unsuitable material has to be factored in as well.

In the best-case scenario children can use social media, appropriate to their age group as a way of:

- Supporting communication
- Sharing information and interests
- Actually setting up face-to-face social activities

But in doing this, they need guidance, support, supervision and positive role models from the adults who care for them. The distinction between 'real' and 'virtual' friends is one that adults can model and guide through their own behaviour.

Limiting time spent communicating with friends online is part of the bigger picture of how you manage your child's use of the internet and time spent sitting in front of a screen.

The Children's Commissioner for England Anne Longfield has criticized the way social media giants draw children into spending more time online. Children now spend more time online than watching television and it's something we parents have to watch carefully. Children aged five to fifteen are now spending an average of fifteen hours a week on the internet. That's a lot, especially for a five-year-old who could be running around outside with a friend.

Anne Longfield drew a useful comparison with food when she said, 'None of us as parents would want our children to eat junk food all the time. For those same reasons we shouldn't want our children to do the same with their online time. When phones, social media and games make us feel worried, stressed and out of control, it means we haven't got the balance right. With your diet, you know that, because you don't feel that good. It's the same with social media.'

You can't ban social media or the internet, nor should you. It's a valuable resource and something all children need to know how to use. The challenge is keeping it in perspective and keeping use moderate.

As with so many other things, the way to limit technology use is to talk to your children about it, explaining the downsides as well as the ups, and to model good use yourself. You can't complain about what they do if you spend all evening on your phone or iPad. So put them away and talk to your children.

Diane says:

As a teacher I worked with children aged five to seven and the differences between girls and boys were always interesting. Girls would use psychological behaviour before physical confrontation – they were far more verbal than the boys and it could be devastating if you were the child on the receiving end.

I used to get girls coming up to me with all sorts of things that other girls had said to them. You can't come to my party. You can't play our game. I'll tell my mum if you won't let me be your friend. We don't like you. The popular children were the ones that the other girls wanted to be friends with, which was partially true with the boys but their play was more physical and involved running around, play-fighting, chasing each other or playing football, and a child on the edge could just run around with them and look as if he was part of the group even if he wasn't. When the girls complained that so and so wouldn't be their friend, I used to tell them that there were plenty of other girls who would be and surely you don't want to be friends with someone who is unkind to you? But acceptance by the 'in-crowd' is very important and this applies at all ages and stages.

I'm so pleased social media was in its infancy when my children were young. I hear stories from friends with teenage children about things that Katie will have to manage with Belle and Penelope. Text messages, trolling, rumour spreading, photo sharing and so on; it seems to be easier to be cruel and unkind when you're hiding behind a computer or phone.

CHAPTER 7

Let Them Be Themselves

Most mums have all kinds of hopes and dreams when their children are born – I certainly did. But the child we get is not always the person we imagined he or she would be. It's easy to picture them becoming a doctor or lawyer, only to find they want to be a surf instructor or a musician. Or we might imagine an outgoing, lively talker, only to find we have a quiet, shy little person.

Perhaps we picture someone just like us, and children are very often not like their parents at all. Or we may hope that they won't be like us at all; that they'll be more adventurous or more high-achieving, only to find that they are just like us and would rather stay at home than aim for a starry career or explore the world.

The trouble is, when we put our expectations onto our children, even if we do it without meaning to, it becomes a pressure on them to be what we would like and not who they really are. That's why sometimes it's important to step back, watch and wait, to see who they are and what they want for themselves. They may be sporty, academic, shy, outgoing, a home-lover or an adventurer, or any one of a thousand other things.

When they're little they change every day and it is impossible to know what direction in life they will choose. But if you nurture who they are, they will blossom and develop confidence, knowing that they are valued and that they have a right to follow their own dreams, no matter how starry or modest those dreams are. And as they grow up, you will have the pleasure of finding out what their choices in life are.

Letting go of some parental expectations and pressures doesn't mean allowing your children to roam wild and free. They need us to show them how to be well-balanced adults who know how to manage their lives and contribute to society. If we can bring them up to be mentally strong, resourceful and self-sufficient, then we can let them fly, when the time comes, knowing that they will be just fine.

So, instead of planning their careers and futures for them, we need to plan for their wellbeing, give them plenty of choices and opportunities, and support them so that they become great adults who enjoy their lives.

No-one will know our children better than we do. We parents and carers will be the ones to see them in different places, times, situations. And we'll be the ones they relate to first. So it's up to us to make sure we have the kind of relationship with them in which they can talk to us about their hopes and wishes and plans, and we will never laugh, never tell them it can't be done or scoff.

121

Instead, we'll applaud their self-belief, offer support and cheer then on from the sidelines.

My Hopes and Dreams

Like every other mother I have plenty of hopes and dreams for my daughters.

I want my girls to be self-sufficient and independent, so that they don't have to rely on a man, or anyone else, for money. I think everyone, woman or man, should be able to make a living and support themselves.

I would never push them into high-paying careers, but I do want stability for them and I want them to have skills that will mean they can always find work.

I see plenty of children around me who are under a lot of pressure to do well at sports, or to be academic and go to university. I don't want my girls to feel that kind of pressure. If they love sports, then great; if they want to go to university, then fine, but I'd be just as happy if they choose not to, as long as they find what it is they want to do in life.

I want Belle and Penelope to feel they can be anything they want to be. And I want their choices to really matter to them. I wouldn't feel that I'd done a good job if they simply wanted to be famous or rich. If they choose a career they love that leads to fame or riches as a by-product, then fine. But fame for fame's sake is empty and disappointing. And money can only go so far. I'd like them to be sensible and careful with money so that they don't worry about it, but that's all.

I would love the girls to have warm, satisfying relationships with partners who love them and who they love in return. Feeling loved is a wonderful thing. I hope the girls will choose partners who respect and care for them. And, while I can't choose their partners, I can try to ensure that Belle and Penelope feel they deserve respect and to be treated well. I want each of them to have a positive self-image and to feel as good as anyone else in their world.

What I don't want is for my girls to be 'nice'. I don't want them to be the kind of women who put their own needs last, who martyr themselves looking after everyone else, who stay silent instead of speaking up or who feel they mustn't cause a fuss. I believe that too many girls, even today, are taught to be 'nice', which so often translates into being a walkover. In many work-places, men get more promotions not because they are better qualified or more able, but because they aren't afraid to speak up, share their ideas (even the bad ones) and ask for what they want. That's because boys are brought up to do this. I want the same for my girls – I don't want them silenced by the pressure to be liked or to be 'good'.

Today's women need to feel they are the equal of anyone, and that they deserve their place at the table, whether that's the board-room table or the kitchen table.

The Unique Self

The reality is that we parents only have limited power over who our children are. We have a lot of influence over them, but we can't decide who they will be – any more than King Canute could hold back the tides. Canute was a Danish Viking King who invaded England a thousand years ago and became ruler of Denmark, England and Norway. Legend has it that he tried – and failed – to hold back the tides. In fact, he was demonstrating to his followers that not even an all-powerful king could command the sea. And it's a fitting comparison, because to a small child a parent is all-powerful, but no parent can hold back their child's individuality or change their unique self.

What Is the Self?

This is a complex question – one that academics, including philosophers, psychologists and theologians have struggled with throughout recorded history. They have pondered over the age-old question of how much in our characters – our unique self – we are born with and how much is due to the environment, including the influence of others. This debate has become known as nature versus nurture and the most recent research on the subject has come to the conclusion that we are the result of both. Which I think any of us with common sense knew already.

Our sense of self comes, to a great degree, from how we believe others view us. If we know we are seen as strong and able, then we feel that we are. But if we perceive others seeing us as weak and ineffective, we will believe that's the way we are.

Self-esteem is the term used to describe how positively individuals view themselves. Again, this may have many aspects and it is perfectly possible, for example, for an individual to have high academic self-esteem, poor social self-esteem and average physical self-esteem or any other combination. It's important to realize that self-esteem is not fixed, it can vary not just from day to day but even from hour to hour or minute to minute.

You can try this out for yourself by rating your own general self-esteem at different points in the day and/or week. Use a simple 1 to 10 rating scale – 10 being the most positive possible and 1 the least positive possible.

Self-knowledge is the degree to which an individual knows and is aware of aspects of themselves. Complete self-knowledge is a lifetime's project, few of us manage it, and children are at a very early stage. But positive and realistic feedback from parents can help a great deal in a child's self-knowledge, and so can well-developed social skills.

Different Stages of Development

Mothers often have a sense of their child's unique self even before birth. Some babies are much more active in the womb and it is even possible to identify patterns of babies' movements across the day and night. Once the baby is born, the child's physical, expressive, emotional, social and behavioural characteristics become more and more evident. And once motor skills and language start to develop, the child can make themselves known to an even greater degree. Everyone has heard of the 'terrible twos', a point in a child's development when their will begins to emerge, sometimes in the form of tantrums and difficult or resistant behaviour. Children begin to know what they want and they can't always manage it or have it, so they get frustrated. Parents need to ride the storm of this period and to be sensitive, creative and patient as much as possible, to avoid storing up even more difficulties when the child reaches adolescence.

The teenage period, during which your child becomes an adult – the process known as adolescence, is the point at which your child's hopes and dreams and choices are most likely to come into conflict with their parents' ideas.

Teenagers have to discover who they are, what is important to them and what they might want to do with their lives. And, on top of everything else, they have to cope with changing bodies and social roles. The options and choices must seem infinite and, understandably, they need to explore and try out different roles and paths. Some young people may have identity and life choices forced upon them by well-meaning parents and carers, which can result in confusion and unhappiness.

Ideally, parents remain calm during this often-turbulent time and can provide a secure base and reference point to which the teenager returns and talks through the inevitable wrong turns and (hopefully) successes. Being able to try, and perhaps fail, and come back and lick their wounds with a non-judgemental parent to talk to is the route to eventually having a secure and positive sense of self.

Choices

A key aspect of letting your children be themselves is giving them choice. For a two-year-old, this might be Toy A or Toy B, but as the child grows older they can make wider choices. Sport is a good example. All children need to be active, but you can give them a choice of activities – for instance, do you want to play hockey, rugby, football, tennis or cricket? So, there's no option about keeping fit, and ideally being part of a team, as this brings with it so many good lessons about sharing and putting the success of the whole team before your own individual success, but your child can choose a sport that appeals to them. You might go along for a tester session of each of the sports to help them choose.

By the time they are in their teens, there are a lot of choices to be made – everything from which clothes to wear to what subjects to study for exams, to who do I want to hang out with, to what career might I like? At this stage, some choices can seem overwhelming and a bit scary, so your job as a parent is to talk all the choices through and be there to offer a sounding board, security and confidence in your child to make the right choice. Plus reminding them that a wrong choice isn't the end of the world.

Top tips for supporting your child in making their own choices:

- Gradually allow your child choices at an age-appropriate level.
- Very young children can usually only cope with a couple of options and these should relate to aspects of their daily life, e.g. toys, games, TV programmes, food.
- As the child ages, offer more choices and, when their understanding and communication has developed sufficiently, let them list options, again, in relation to the range of their daily life.
- As children become older, the influence of peers will increase. Sometimes the friends your children choose will

not be the ones you would choose for them but this is a reflection of their unique identity and has to be worked with. You may not agree to support contact out of school but at school it will be up to them who they relate to and choose to play with.

- When the teenage years arrive, your children will be influenced by the current youth culture. Appearance, friendships, use of leisure time will all be aspects of their lives that they push to have more control over. As a parent, you are focused upon keeping them safe, ensuring their health and overall wellbeing and supporting their learning and development in general. Try to enable them in making wise choices through your own example and in day-to-day conversations and shared activities but realize that you need to pick your battles and reach compromise as much as possible.

- Young adulthood seems to be extending nowadays with children staying in the family home for longer than in previous generations. Their education and career aspirations and choices may not be the ones that you would choose for them and they certainly can't be expected to reflect and live out your own dreams, fulfilled or otherwise. This may be a source of disappointment or even disapproval but it is important that you have a relationship in which their individuality is respected and communicated. If you achieve this, then there is more chance that they will discuss their aims and life choices with you and then be able to use your own hard-earned life experience and the fact that you are there for them whenever they need you.

EXERCISE: RECOGNIZING YOUR TEENAGER'S STRENGTHS

There is likely to come a time when your child's choices run counter to what you would like. For example, your daughter who has always shown great musical promise and has learned to play the piano to a good standard suddenly decides to give up her piano lessons because she just wants to hang out with friends. You might feel that you have failed in some way as a parent and think she has 'gone off the rails'.

The more you try to encourage her to get back to her music, the more resistant she is. Every strategy you've tried is unsuccessful; encouragement, discussion, nagging, outright arguments and even grounding and removing pocket money or computer privileges. It can begin to feel as though the daughter you know has disappeared and been replaced by someone you don't much like.

At this point, it is really important to focus on her strengths – reminding yourself, and your daughter, what they are. That may feel like a real effort, but it will really help you and your teenager through what is so often a turbulent time.

Why should you be so positive?
- You need to feel positive about all the parenting you've offered so far and about your child's individuality, courage and wish to make their own choices.
- You may understand your teenager better and be able

to understand their viewpoint more clearly, and in this way mutual trust is more likely to grow.

- Your love and acceptance is needed to support your teenager's self-esteem.
- Communication will continue rather than shut down. If you meet your child's resistance with more resistance, it is hard to find and reach compromises and the only thing that results is a power struggle.
- Home and family life will be much easier and more peaceful.

If you are struggling to even remember what your child's strengths are, follow these steps:

- Choose three things about your teenager that you consider to be strengths. Think about their social, physical, emotional and learning characteristics, their creativity, resilience, courage, tenacity ... the potential list is endless.
- For the next month, try to notice when these strengths are apparent and in what situations.
- Note any positive changes in behaviour and what your son or daughter communicates, both verbally and non-verbally.
- Acknowledge and give yourself a treat for staying positive and reflect on how you can use this experience to build your relationship with your child.
- After a month, ask yourself:
  What have been the gains?
  Is your relationship any closer?

How has your understanding developed?

Have there been any unexpected benefits, perhaps changes to other relationships in your life?

Aisha and Gita's Story

When her daughter Aisha was born, Gita hoped that she would grow up to make a happy marriage, have children and keep a warm and comfortable home for her family. This was what Gita had done, and her mother and grandmother before her; it was the family expectation of daughters.

Gita and her husband Deepak also had an older son, Hari, and they hoped that he would grow up to be a doctor or a lawyer. Deepak had worked hard all his life as a bus driver, but he wanted his son to have a profession.

By the time Aisha was twelve and Hari was fifteen, it was clear that things were not going according to plan. Hari did not like school very much and he didn't want to be either a doctor or a lawyer. He loved playing cricket and football with his friends, he was a talented guitarist and he wanted to be in a rock band. Aisha, on the other hand, loved to study, she was top of her class and keen to go to university to study science.

Gita and Deepak were dismayed and puzzled by both their children. They did their best to get Hari to study – which led to a lot of family rows – and they steered Aisha towards home-making skills, insisting that she cook every weekend with her mother, even though she had no interest at all in cooking.

At eighteen, after many rows, Hari left home and cut off contact with his parents. Gita and Deepak were heartbroken. They realized they had pushed him too hard and they regretted how rigid their expectations had been. All they wanted was to have Hari home and to know he was safe.

Because they had lost one child, they stopped trying to force Aisha down the domestic path. She shone in her exams and won a place at university to study Biology. Her dream was to work in medical research. During her second year, Hari, now twenty-two, reappeared in their lives. He was well and happy and working as a trainee chef, a job he loved.

Gita and Deepak were overjoyed to have a second chance, having come close to losing their son and possibly their daughter too. It took effort to overturn their very fixed expectations, but they took the decision to accept their children's choices in life, rather than risk alienating them.

Enable Them to Thrive

Thriving is all about the quality of life, rather than the specifics of what you do and achieve. It's about flourishing, being well and strong, confident and resilient. It's loving life and living it to the full, feeling comfortable and at ease with yourself and who you are.

So how do we help our children to thrive?

As a starting point, ask yourself what you want most for your child. Is it to excel in maths, to become prime minister or to win a gold medal? Very few parents would actually give this kind of answer. Most would say they want their children to be happy. And when you break happiness down, it consists of things like:

- Being involved in activities that bring you pleasure
- Having good relationships with others
- Being kind and generous
- Feeling that you make a contribution
- Doing work that feels fulfilling and worthwhile

Enabling your child to thrive really comes down to giving them the space and time and opportunities to find out what they really love to do – more than one thing, hopefully – and then supporting them in following their passion.

This doesn't mean letting them try something new every week. It's important that they learn to stick at things and give anything they start a fair chance. And it doesn't mean filling every hour of their day with new activities. Packing the after-school hours with endless clubs can be exhausting for you and your child.

To find out who they are, what they love and what gives them meaning in life, your child needs plenty of space. Time to themselves, time spent in nature, time spent chatting or reading or going camping with friends.

Don't worry too much about outcomes, or how they're going to make a living. Too much focus on this creates huge pressure and that stifles creativity, freedom and ideas. Trust that they will find the right way to make a living once they find what gives them joy in life and what makes them want to get up in the morning. Even if this isn't something that leads to an obvious career, let them go for it – you may well be surprised where it will take them.

Make Them Mentally Strong

It's our job as parents to help our children become mentally strong. That means bringing out the best in them and equipping them to manage the world and feel good about themselves and life.

These are some of the things that will help:

- **Have interests you enjoy in your own life:** There's nothing like showing them how it's done. Whether you help out with the local church or sing in a choir or go to exercise classes, do things that you enjoy and show your child what that gives you and why you stick with it. It's also important that you don't make your children the centre of your universe, otherwise they'll grow up thinking everyone should cater to their needs. Having interests of your own is part of this.
- **When your child finds something they like doing, support them in it:** Help them make it happen. Drive them to the lessons or practices, get them the equipment, look for a local teacher or club, and show your child you're backing them.
- **Hold back on criticism, doubt and cynicism:** OK, so the first violin recital sounds like a strangled cat, the gym demonstration ends in a tumble – and tears, the first match ends with a sending-off – or spending most

of it on the sidelines as a sub. No matter, these are early steps and what your child needs from you is a big hug, a confidence-boosting bit of praise and faith that it's worth sticking in there.

- **Give them responsibility:** Right from the start, give them jobs to do around the house. A three-year-old can help set the table, put socks away in a drawer and tidy away toys. As they get a bit older, they need to help with jobs that are for the whole family – cooking, washing up, cleaning the bathroom, and they also need to begin taking responsibility for their own things. Expect your children to look after their own sports kit, getting it ready before a lesson or match. They can also get their schoolbag ready, make their own packed lunches and tidy their rooms. Children who perform age-appropriate duties aren't overburdened, they're gaining skills they need to become responsible adults.

- **Let them make mistakes:** Don't correct their homework for them, remind them to do their chores or double-check that they've remembered their books or kit. Children need to face the consequences of mistakes – if they don't, then adulthood comes as a shock. We all mess up and we all have to deal with it. When you learn from mistakes you become wiser and stronger.

- **Separate consequences from punishment:** Consequences are about teaching children how to do better in future, while punishment is making them suffer for doing something wrong. Enforcing consequences is far more effective.

135

For instance, your child doesn't tidy her room, which she needs to do to earn her pocket money. So she doesn't get her pocket money. That's a consequence and the chances are she will tidy her room next time. Your job done.

- **Encourage your child to work once they reach their teens:** Earning your own money is a great feeling, work gives meaning to life and knowing how to work – including turning up on time and putting in the hours – is a valuable life skill. So, get them to look for ways to earn their own income. Car washing, a Saturday job, babysitting, making crafts to sell – there are lots of things that teenagers can do to start earning.

- **Finally – and perhaps most importantly – teach your children to focus on what they can offer the world, rather than what they can gain from it:** Service is an old-fashioned term, but a good concept. Do something to help other people, animals, your community or nature – help clean up the local park, walk a sick neighbour's dog, get involved in community groups. It's a great way to bring up children who aren't too self-absorbed.

Diane says:

We always wanted our children to be themselves and to do what they loved. Katie's dad and I recently saw a documentary about a school that experimented with 'No boys, no girls'. The school already thought they treated girls the same as the boys but this programme went a bit further and explored how the children felt about being a boy or girl and how this influenced their behaviour. It made us think about the way we all consciously or sub-consciously influence our children's choices as they grow up.

We shared roles in the home and I hope we were good role models in this respect for our three and I believe they have all grown up with the expectation that they are equal to their partners and there shouldn't be things that only men or women can do, in the home and in the world of work.

They all had a good range of toys to play with. Paul could play with dolls and Katie and Suzy could play with trains and cars. And they did just that, although I think nature wins eventually as they all gradually spent more time with traditional boys' or girls' toys as they got older. But they were never made to feel it was wrong to choose one toy above another.

I can see that Katie shares this attitude too as Belle had a tool kit with a drill which she loved, a doctor's kit (not a nurse's outfit) which she still loves, cars, trains and dinosaurs, a Batman dressing-up outfit and a superheroes T-shirt. But, despite all this, at the age of three she started gravitating towards the princess dresses, refused to wear trousers and said her favourite colour was pink! It will be interesting to see if Penelope is the same.

CHAPTER

Trauma

About half of us will face a traumatic event in our lives, either directly or as a witness. This is a major, stressful and emotionally overwhelming event, which has a lasting impact on us. We may be a bystander, for instance those witnessing a terrorist attack, or it may happen to us directly, for example being assaulted or involved in a serious accident.

Traumatic events include natural or man-made disasters, such as a hurricane, flood, fire or earthquake. They can include car accidents, all kinds of physical and sexual assaults, robberies and violence. And they can include life-threatening illness and sudden bereavement.

The effects of being involved in or closely witnessing a traumatic event can be profound. Immediately after the event, feelings of numbness, shock and denial are typical. Longer-term reactions can include unpredictable emotions, flashbacks, strained relationships and physical symptoms like headaches and nausea. And while we very often cope, in practical terms, with whatever has happened, it can leave lasting psychological scars. For every person who goes through a massive trauma, there is a family adjusting to it and struggling with disbelief, guilt and grief.

Traumatic events are, by their nature, terrifying, and they cause us physical, emotional, spiritual or psychological harm. These events undermine our sense of self, they rock our mental and emotional stability and cause us to see the world differently. Healing can take a long time and a lot of patience.

Not everyone involved in or witnessing a traumatic event necessarily suffers trauma. But many people do and the effects can be long-lasting and require specialist help. But there is also a lot that we can do to help ourselves and our children to overcome the after-effects of trauma.

Sometimes the traumatic events are hidden, and the resulting trauma can be hard to spot. I'm talking in particular about sexual abuse in children – a traumatic event that happens in secret, usually with no witnesses. It's something every parent dreads happening to their child, but since it can happen in so many situations it's vital that we all know how to spot the signs and what to do.

Trauma can linger a long time, and in its most severe and chronic form a condition called post-traumatic stress can develop. Distressing emotional responses, such as anxiety, fear and depression, are symptoms of post-traumatic stress disorder, which, if left untreated, can continue over months or even years.

It's important for parents to spot the signs that a child may have experienced trauma, so that professional help can be found. There are also many children's books that cover this topic that might be helpful.

The symptoms may include any or all of the following:

- Re-experiencing the trauma through intrusive thoughts, flashbacks, dreams about the event or suddenly feeling that the traumatic event is re-occurring
- A blankness or numbing of responsiveness to everyday life in the form of decreased interest in activities, people or situations, feeling detached from others or reduced feelings in general
- Sleep disturbance
- Being easily startled
- Expressions of guilt about surviving the event where others have not
- Concentration and memory problems
- Avoiding activities

Trauma in My Life

The traumatic event that happened to me is well documented. My life changed in an instant when industrial-strength acid was thrown in my face by a stranger. He was instructed to do it by a man I had dated a handful of times. When this man realized I wanted to stop seeing him, he locked me in a hotel room and raped me. He threatened to kill me and I was too afraid to go to the police, so I stayed in my flat, numb with shock. Four days later came the acid attack. The man who threw it waited until I finally ventured out.

I was left badly injured and close to death. The acid ate into my face, neck, arm, ear, eye and internally into my throat and oesophagus. I went through many months of skin grafts and operations, physiotherapy and rehabilitation. I was cared for by extraordinary medical staff and by my parents, who were dedicated and wonderful. I, and those closest to me, inevitably suffered traumatic shock.

What came out of it for me was a determination not to be beaten – not to let the bad guys win. They injured me physically, but they couldn't touch my spirit. Knowing that got me through the worst of days.

My mum, Diane, had to cope as a parent, along with my dad, David. I was only twenty-four, I still thought everyone in the world was my friend, I was confident and trusting and full of dreams and hopes. My mum and dad had to see me brought very low, physically and mentally, and they helped me to recover. It was the toughest thing anyone could ask of a parent. What they went through very few parents have had to go through. I wasn't aware of just how tough it was for them, at the time, but I learned about it when I recovered, by reading Mum's diaries and talking to her.

I'm going to hand over to Mum to talk about that time – we both hope that by talking about her side of things she will perhaps help other mothers coping with tragedy to feel less alone and less afraid of the future.

Diane's Story: Extracts from My Diaries

Monday 31 March 2008

Around 6.30pm we received the phone call from the police that was to impact on all our lives for ever. Katie had been the victim of a 'chemical attack'. They couldn't give us a lot of detail. What did they mean by a chemical attack? How badly was she hurt? We had to phone the hospital for more information and they told us she had burns to her face, neck and chest and was at the Royal Free Hospital Hampstead. They said they weren't going to keep her there, so I hoped that meant it wasn't too serious. We didn't know what to think, I couldn't imagine what chemical it was.

We rapidly packed some bags and headed from our home in Andover, Hampshire, to north London. We got to the Royal Free at about 9pm. There in a waiting room were Katie's five flatmates. We spoke to them briefly, and then waited for what seemed an eternity until a doctor came to talk to us. We were taken into the room where she was lying heavily sedated, her face swollen to the size of a football, her lips swollen, her tongue protruding from her mouth and a ventilator helping her breathe. The room was silent except for the noise of the machines keeping her alive. A doctor was washing her face and eyes, trying to neutralize whatever had been thrown on her. They told us she was going be transferred to a specialist burns unit in the Chelsea and Westminster Hospital.

They brought her out to a waiting ambulance, her face covered by a cloth to protect it. We weren't allowed to travel with her so we watched while it went off into the night with its blue light flashing.

We followed, arriving at about midnight. We went up to the

burns unit on the fifth floor and were taken straight to see her in the intensive care ward of the unit. She had been heavily sedated and put into a type of sit-in shower to be washed.

I don't think I could take anything in; I can't remember any of the doctors' names or faces. I don't remember the nurses or anything they said to us. I just remember the extremely bright lights and the heat – burns units have to be kept very warm.

The last time we had seen Katie was on Mother's Day, a few weeks earlier. She'd come down by train to see us. She had been sharing a flat, working in London, full of stories about her life. A week or two later I'd had a text saying she had a new boyfriend. Now this. I couldn't take it in. She was twenty-four, just a normal girl, living her life.

After about an hour we were shown to a relatives' room with a single bed and a mattress on the floor. I lay on the mattress, fully clothed, and David got into the bed. I just lay there immobile; I didn't cry, I just kept thinking 'Oh my God' over and over again. I thought if I lay there long enough without moving then I would fall asleep but of course I didn't. My mind was racing. Our lives would never be the same again. Katie's life was over; how could she exist without a face? It had been destroyed. She had no future, we had no future. I would give up work, she would live with us, I'd have to look after her for ever . . . what if she was blind? More and more scenarios went round and round in my head.

Tuesday 1 April 2008
At 6am there was a knock on the door. My heart leapt – what had happened? Had she died? It was a nurse telling us that Katie

wanted to see us. I couldn't believe it, she was conscious and able to communicate? It seemed like a miracle.

We went straight to her bedside. We said her name and touched her. She knew we were there but she couldn't open her eyes, they seemed welded together. She couldn't speak. She was intubated and had an oxygen mask over her face. She could move her head slightly and she nodded when I spoke to her. Her face was black, brown and orange. Large pieces seemed to be bubbling up and flaking off. She was totally unrecognizable.

The nurse had given her some paper on a clipboard and a pen. She was writing things to us. She wrote, 'Help me, I can't breathe. Where am I? Am I dead? Am I blind? I'm sorry. I love you. Please don't cry.' I asked, 'Did he do this to you?' and she nodded her head and started to cry. We sat with her all day, she tried to speak but her voice was rasping and gruff. She kept on writing . . . telling us dreadful things that had happened to her. How she had been attacked and raped, how he was mixed up with guns and had threatened to kill her, she was terrified that he would come to the hospital to kill her. One of the most upsetting things she wrote was 'Kill me.' She wanted to die now rather than wait for him to come and finish her off.

I am writing this many months on from those early days and looking back it seems almost surreal. As if it was a film I'd watched or a dream I'd had. In fact, it was horribly real and almost too traumatic to take in. I kept a diary of important events: operations, police interviews, clinic visits, in case anyone needed to know such things. A lot happened that I didn't document: the waiting around; stopping doctors in corridors hoping for any tiny pieces of information; not being able to sleep properly, waking up and hoping it was morning and finding out I'd only been asleep for an hour; David going to the hospital chapel to pray every morning, I went once but didn't get any comfort from it; those times when the tension and stress got too much and we snapped at each other and rowed about things I can't remember; standing at the window and being amazed that people were going about their daily lives while we were suffering so much.

Katie's Forty-five Days in Hospital

The police had arranged for Katie to do a photo ID parade on a laptop. This was going to happen in the afternoon. We were very worried that Katie was getting sleepier as the day wore on. We let her sleep as long as we dared, then tried to keep her awake by showing her newspaper pictures and 'get well' cards. This ID was such an important thing we couldn't risk her getting it wrong. We were worried about her eyesight, which had been affected. We kept showing her pictures of famous people asking her who they were. Two people arrived: a solicitor and a policeman who used the laptop. It was explained that one of us could stay in the room as long as we were out of her eye line and couldn't see the pictures on the screen. She would see nine faces and she wasn't to say anything until all nine were shown, and then she would see them again and would be asked if she could pick out the man who had thrown the acid at her. David said he would stay with Katie.

Afterwards he said that, although he couldn't see the screen, he could see her face and when one particular picture was shown he says a look of pure terror crossed her face. He said it was dreadful

145

to see and something he will remember for the rest of his life. Her terror was so extreme that she lost control of her bowels. She said, 'Dad, I've messed myself' and started crying. The solicitor who had previously said there was to be no contact was so moved that he told David to go and comfort her. Despite all this she still carried on with the ID parade and picked out the man responsible.

One little memory that seems trivial looking back on it was the day before her major skin graft. The doctor had said he would take the skin from her back. I remember that evening she was sitting in her chair and she leaned forward to get something and the back of her gown fell open. As I went to tie it up for her I stroked the smooth, unblemished skin of her back and thought how sad that the next day it would be scarred too.

After this skin graft, Katie was put into an induced coma to keep her stable. David and I now had more time on our hands, although we were still meeting regularly with the police. We walked up and down the local streets and drank endless cups of coffee. We talked constantly about the situation but (and I'm hoping this is a correct memory) we were never despairing. We had so many people supporting us, keeping us informed, letting us ask questions and always being there for us so I believe we felt reassured and hopeful. Katie's surgeon had told us to take one day at a time, not to worry about the future, to concentrate on the day. This was good advice; the future was so bewildering, so uncertain, and it wasn't good to dwell on things we had no control over. We had to concentrate on what we could do that particular day; we would cope with tomorrow when it came. The staff wanted us to go home for a few days but we couldn't leave her. Sometimes Paul and Suzy, her brother and sister, came to spend a couple of hours with us. We tried to be normal but by then they had both realized the seriousness of the situation so it was often a subdued get-together. But it helped to have them around; I believe the family should rally round and support each other in times like these.

When the doctors decided to wake her up, they gradually reduced the drugs and we had some very scary moments. She became very confused and had hallucinations, she tried to get out of bed and we had to help the nurses to restrain her. She was fighting us and shouting and we had to hold her down while she was sedated. We could see in her eyes that she was absolutely terrified; she obviously thought she was being attacked again. We found it really hard to cope with that and were very upset. Although our heads knew it was the reaction to the drugs, our hearts were breaking seeing the terror on her face as if we were the attackers. We were very shaken up and felt so guilty that we were inadvertently causing her so much anguish.

In the burns unit, they don't have any mirrors so she had absolutely no idea what she looked like. Early on she had said to us, 'What do I look like then?' and we'd had to hide our distress. All the skin on her face had been removed, to avoid infection and she had pieces of donated skin, all different colours, stapled together to protect her face until they could do the grafts. She asked us to draw a picture, so David did, and Katie laughed and said, 'I look like a patchwork quilt.' She still had her sense of humour and I marvelled at that.

When the time came for her to see herself, a few weeks later, we went into a room with the psychologist. The psychologist said you have got to remember this is how you look now, not what you are going to end up like. The best thing to do is to look at the scars on your chest and maybe up to your chin or mouth, but don't look at your whole face. We both thought, we know Katie, that's not how she's going to do it. They gave her a hand mirror and of course she put it straight up to her face and gave out the most horrific scream imaginable. To this day, I can remember the noise. She burst into tears saying, 'I don't want to live my life like a freak.' Even the psychologist looked upset.

I think Katie hit absolute rock bottom at that point. There were a few days when she didn't want to know, wouldn't get out of bed, she was never going to go outside again . . . we went through dreadful times in that short period. She couldn't see a way forward and she became suicidal.

Then something changed. Katie was thinking about ending her life and she was crying, when she felt a warm rush come over her and she heard a voice saying, 'Don't worry, everything is going to be alright.' She thought it was an angel visiting her and it gave her the courage to fight back. She changed her mind about giving in and she said, 'I'm not going to let that man win, I'm going to get through this. I'm going to be the winner.'

Katie was discharged on 15 May, after forty-five days in hospital. She came back home with us and from then on it was our job to look after her. At that stage she couldn't even walk, she was bent double, from her injuries and the length of time she had spent in bed and on heavy drugs. We had to practise walking with her, up and down the corridors.

June 2008

Our days are regulated by face care and eye drops and hospital visits. Sometimes it's hard to get Katie out of bed in the morning. It's so important that she has the massage and does her face exercises but she gets stroppy when we try to get her up. Her first lot of eye drops have to be done at around 7am, it's so hard getting her to open her eyes wide enough especially as she has to sleep with the mask on. She tells me to go away and refuses to open her eyes. It's like she was a sulky teenager again. But then we don't know what kind of night she has had; she doesn't sleep well, she has nightmares and flashbacks and often isn't in the right frame of mind for face care when I go in. It's hard for all of us really. David and I want to do the right thing for her recovery and do the eye drops and massage but we also have to think of her emotional recovery too and that is the bit we can't see and find the hardest to deal with. There are days with lots of tears but then again there are days when she is incredibly upbeat. Sometimes she'll go up to her room and I can hear her crying and I don't know what to do. Her psychologist, Lisa, has said we must let her cry. She needs to release her emotions, but as a mum I just want to comfort her . . . she's my child, I want to make her better but I can't. I have to learn to stand back. She has to feel able to express her anger, hurt and pain in any way she wants.

We have to deal with our feelings too. We massage her face three times a day, you have to stretch the grafted skin until it turns white. David and I take turns doing it and sometimes when one of us is massaging her the other goes into the next room to cry. We never cry in front of her.

One of the doctors, Mr Jawad, had said to us, 'What you have to do is stop thinking about what she is going to do tomorrow, next week or next month. You have to think of a day at a time, of tiny steps, every day is a step forward.' That was a great help, we were overthinking things and we had to stop.

Katie is being fed through a tube, she can't eat. She sleeps with a machine next to her bed to help her breathe. If it gets air in it an alarm goes off. One night it went off and David leaped out of bed to go to her and ran into the wall. It's like having a baby again.

July 2008

Katie has been home for about two months now.

Sometimes it's like treading on eggshells; we can't say anything right. We get accused of being patronising or not caring enough. Sometimes there's no answer . . . and really Katie doesn't want an answer she just wants to let off steam and we are first in the firing line! We have to be very strong and realize that she is not having a go at us personally; she is attacking the situation and letting out her frustration and anger. Who else can she let it out on after all? I know I shouldn't let it get to me, I know why she's shouting and yelling but my heart still hurts and it feels so personal. I need to stay calm but it's hard to see someone you love so much being so aggressive and in so much turmoil. Katie's mask is pressing on her teeth, causing her pain so that doesn't help.

The knock-on effect of all this sends ripples through the whole family. Suzy is unhappy in her job and her relationship with her boyfriend has broken down. She is unsure how to act around Katie and feels she can't confide in us as we have enough to contend with.

I am trying to coordinate different clinics . . . eye clinic at Chelsea and Westminster; eye clinic at Great Western; burns unit at C & W; Iain at St George's for mask and Dr Benson at Endoscopy for her throat. It just seems endless and it affects us all in one way or another. We all have our own problems to work through. Katie tries to be so positive most of the time so we have to stay strong for her and not show it if we get upset. It is unfair to her as she is the one suffering the most. We have to let her rant and rave, be happy or sad, stay in her PJs all day if she wants to. I know that no matter what she shouts at us, it's a result of what happened to her. Funnily enough sometimes I'm glad she feels safe enough to let it out on us. She knows that, no matter what, we will never desert her or stop loving her and when we come out of all this we will be stronger than ever.

Over the Following Months . . .
When we heard that Katie was able to go to France for treatment we were so excited and yet also very worried about her being there on her own (especially with her poor schoolgirl French!). She was unable to stay for long periods as she had to keep coming back for her eye and throat operations and the legal trial, so it was a case of fitting in short stays. David and I went with her the first time and stayed in a hotel in the village so we were able to meet up with her in the evenings. I also went with her a couple of times but the time came when she said she was prepared to go on her own. How she found the courage to do that I do not know. But she did. She put up with the stares, the whispered comments, the questioning from airport officials. She got herself

to and from the airport and clinic and she coped with the food, the treatment, the language and the lonely evenings. Her bravery never ceased to amaze me. She would phone us every evening with all the news and would make us laugh with her stories. She can always find something amusing in every situation. It did her good physically and mentally. She was always so excited about the treatment she was having and we really looked forward to welcoming her back home and discussing the positive changes she could see on her face.

We keep a photographic record of the changes and improvements. It was Katie's idea and it helps, because she can see how she used to look and that there is steady progress.

When Channel 4 heard what had happened and asked to film Katie for a documentary, we thought it would involve an interview. In fact, they filmed one day a week for six months. The women making the film, Jessie and another Katie, were brilliant. They were Katie's age and they got on well with her – they used to talk for hours. They wanted to make the documentary positive and uplifting. They encouraged Katie to do things she thought weren't possible, like walking to the shops alone.

As Katie gradually recovered, she began to say, 'How will I earn money? What will I do?' I remember feeling hopeless, I didn't know what to say to her. I suggested she could stay at home, perhaps find a job locally, but that was never Katie. After two years at home, she decided to move to a flat in London. She was scared, but she was determined to do it. She put bolts and chains on her front door and we were relieved when we heard there was a policeman living downstairs and he told her she could call him anytime.

We worried, of course we did, and we still do. But Katie turned a tragic situation around and has made a success of her life. And she's a remarkable person. We are immensely proud of her. We always will be.

Looking Back

There's an awful lot of what Mum and Dad describe to me about those early days that I don't remember at all. I was living in a world of fear and pain – the world I knew had ended and I didn't know what, if anything, was coming next. I was completely traumatized and so were my family. It's only looking back that I realize how tough it was for them. I'm incredibly grateful for their steadfast love and support. Mum and Dad spent hours every day, for many months, nursing and caring for me and they managed to stay strong, but I know they shed a lot of tears too.

As a family I think it made us stronger. The bond between us is very precious and I'm proud of how my parents and brother and sister have coped.

My parents have since been able to offer support to other parents going through similar levels of distress and trauma. That's something incredibly valuable to have come out of it all. I have mentored many other traumatized burns survivors through my charity, The Katie Piper Foundation, and my parents have helped other families. We can pass on what we learned and went through and, most importantly, the message that there is hope, there is life after serious trauma. Just take a day at a time, look for small improvements and stay as positive as you can.

I received counselling from the start and it has been a lifeline for me. I couldn't have got through without the support of the counsellors who have helped me to make sense of events, to keep perspective and to find my path forward.

Treatment and Counselling

It is essential to look for professional help if you believe that your child or teenager is showing symptoms that may have arisen as a result of trauma. If the right support is not sought, there can be repercussions for a child or young person's overall development and learning as well as their general wellbeing. Research is making more and more connections between the effects of trauma and neurological development, health and behaviour. Your GP is likely to be the first port of call unless there have been physical injuries which have necessitated medical help, in which case you should have medical professionals on hand from whom you can seek advice if you think that post-trauma help is needed.

Children who have experienced trauma have often subsequently benefited from various therapeutic approaches, such as play, music, drama or art therapy. Children's capacities to work through emotional and psychological difficulties through these different but always individualized methods practised by skilled therapists can be awe-inspiring.

Some ideas for you as parent to help your child who has suffered trauma:

- Make opportunities for 'unforced' conversations, which are led by the child or young person. Often these can accompany everyday activities or play. Car journeys where you are driving and your child is a passenger can be helpful because there is not so much face-to-face contact!
- Be led by your child's wishes. Ask them how you can help best.
- *Listen.*
- Make space and time for privacy when talking about the difficult experience.
- Reassure them that the difficult feelings will pass in time and are perfectly natural and understandable. Also be reassured that every person who goes through a trauma will have their own process of and stages of grief.
- Try not to avoid the taboo subjects – be honest in reply to their direct questions.
- Watch out for the 'red flags' in your child's behaviour and emotions such as fear, guilt, anger and deep sadness, and seek support when these are prolonged and deep.
- Use books, music, stories and games to distract and calm, especially at night when there are usually fewer activities and everyday distractions to help stop their ruminations.
- Encourage and support contact with friends so that your child avoids becoming socially isolated.
- Talk to the child's school about what has happened and if necessary ask for some support from the school's educational psychologist or, if they have one, the school counsellor.

CHAPTER 9

Managing Anxiety

All of us know what it is to feel anxious. Who hasn't felt apprehensive, worried or uneasy about something that's happening or is anticipated in our lives? Even the most confident people become anxious sometimes, and for most of us this isn't a problem – anxiety is a normal response to certain events or thoughts and it passes. But for others it can become a way of life, fixated around fears that may never come true, dominating our waking hours and depriving us of sleep.

Many adults grapple with anxiety in a world that is becoming more and more pressurized, but it is also increasing alarmingly fast in children too. Recent research indicates that as many as one in six young people between the ages of six and fifteen will experience severe anxiety – which might include exam stress, social anxiety, panic attacks or obsessive compulsive disorder (OCD).

Anxiety is especially high among girls. Experts estimate that a third of all teenage girls in the UK suffer from anxiety and depression. And one in five girls is self-harming – an alarming number. This stratospheric level of anxiety is a new trend in the past ten years or so. Before that, things had been getting better for girls for a hundred years, as opportunities opened up and the fight for equality meant girls had more choices in life than ever before. But the combination of social media and the pressure and competition girls now face to be top in exams, to get great jobs, to look hot and act cool, has led to many girls growing up too fast and worrying constantly.

Excessive anxiety can lead to serious mental health problems, so it's important to spot it as early as possible and to get the right help. But how do you know when the problem is serious, and when it's simply a normal part of growing up? You can't stop your child from worrying at all, so how much worry is alright, and how much is, well, worrying?

As girls and boys approach their teenage years they have to navigate the pitfalls of growing up with their lives in the spotlight of Instagram, Facebook and Snapchat. Added to that, there is their blossoming and sometimes confused sexuality, and the need to find relationships and jobs.

Children today are also more aware than ever of how dangerous and unpredictable the world can be, as the news brings terrorism, plane crashes and disasters to their doorsteps. So how do you talk to them about all these things? What do you do if anxiety seems to be spiralling out of control? And how do you help your child to manage anxiety and develop resilience?

What Is Anxiety?

Anxiety is an umbrella term used to describe feelings of apprehension, fear, worry and nervousness. The term anxiety, like many terms used to describe our mental, emotional and physical state is one that comes from medical terminology but is used so frequently in everyday life that its original meaning has become defused and weakened.

Anxiety can actually be a useful and necessary way to feel as it can help us to keep safe and to avoid and manage risks and threats. If we didn't feel anxious, we wouldn't choose to be cautious in uncertain situations, or to resolve worries, or to keep out of the way of danger.

Anxiety can even enhance performance: worrying before a business meeting, a stage appearance or a presentation is natural and can keep us sharp and bring out our strengths.

The words anxiety and stress are often used together or interchangeably, and we can certainly suffer from both at the same time, but the term stress is properly used to describe the physical response to real or perceived threat, difficulty and danger, while anxiety in the mind.

In evolutionary terms, anxiety is a manifestation of the well-known 'fight or flight' response. Thousands of years ago, early humans needed to identify and manage risk on a daily basis in order to survive. The appearance of a sabre-toothed tiger meant you either got away to safety or stood and fought. Nowadays, such extreme threat is thankfully very rare. However, there are many potential and actual situations that cause a milder 'fight or flight' sequence of responses, where you become aware of threats to your wellbeing, which then arouse negative uncomfortable feelings, triggering a release of hormones in your body, causing your breathing and heart rate to rise and various other physical changes such as sweating, a change of body temperature or trembling.

Examples of situations that are likely to provoke anxiety include:

- Drinking too much coffee or caffeine-laden drinks like cola
- Running late for an appointment, work or some other commitment
- Travelling delays and problems
- Receiving bad news, e.g. an unexpected and large bill or information about a relative or friend's health problems
- Making a mistake
- Being involved in an accident

However, anxiety can also be triggered by something that hasn't yet happened or by imagining the worst. Most parents of older children know the feelings of intense anxiety that can arise if your child is late home, stranded somewhere, or if you can't contact them. It's all too easy to imagine alarming scenarios, only to have all your fears dissolve as soon as your child walks through the door.

My Anxiety Journey

I was never an anxious child or teenager. My world was safe and comfortable, my parents were solid and secure, and I wasn't a natural worrier. In fact, until I was twenty-four I was so laid-back that I seldom thought anything could go wrong. I felt that whatever I did was going to work out just fine and I loved meeting new people, trying new things and going to new places.

I was always thirsting for new adventures and longing to travel the world and try everything.

All that changed with the attack. Afterwards, I became extremely anxious and acutely aware of every risk and potential danger. It was part of my response to the trauma I experienced. I was left with post-traumatic stress disorder (PTSD) and anxiety was a huge part of this.

Over the years, I have worked hard to manage my anxiety, but it's not something I can completely cure. On the anxiety scale, I've gone from one extreme to the other and now it's a never-ending journey of coping mechanisms and strategies, recognizing triggers and working on ways of calming myself.

Through my charity, I meet a lot of traumatized people. In any one week, I might meet ten people who have recently been injured in household accidents, car crashes or fires caused by something as small as a dodgy charger bought from a market stall. And while my work as a mentor and the charity's power to sponsor treatment has meant such a lot to me, meeting people who have suffered in this way has probably reinforced my own trauma. It has certainly made me even more risk aware. Ironically, I've become the person who would have irritated the old me. I was a thrill-seeker, now I'd be pointing out the risks and dangers and urging caution, even as the old me was saying, 'I don't care.'

I'm not sure that any mental health issue should be contained

– I believe it should be expressed and acknowledged and worked through, so I don't try to control or contain my anxiety. Knowing that there isn't always a solution or cure can help with acceptance, and I do try to accept the way I am and not beat myself up about it. I will always have a high level of anxiety because something bad has happened to me and the memory of it can't be eradicated. But I can manage it so that it doesn't impact on my life too badly, and although I do have bad days, I have good ones too.

A bad day might be brought on by something external, like hearing about a terrorist attack in London. Or it might be something internal – my worry over being late for an appointment, for instance. Of course, that's not the end of the world, but for me the anxiety is triggered by feeling out of control of the situation. I want to be on time and, because of a traffic jam or some other thing, I can't.

I can also feel very low if some small thing goes wrong – a prospective job not working out, for example. I can be logical about the reasons for it but it can still trigger a lot of anxiety in me about the future.

I know that my anxiety is fuelled by my inner critic, the voice inside my head that tells me I should have got it 'right', so I try to pause that tape, step back and get perspective on the situation. I'll tell myself these things happen all the time, it isn't personal, look at all the times things do work out just fine – that kind of thing.

I also remind myself that I have been in really bad situations and this is definitely not one of them. I'll tell myself, you got through that, so the traffic jam and the job hitch aren't so bad.

Damage limitation is important, so if I'm anxious and stressed about a call or an email or something I need to tackle, I will get off my emails or phone and remind myself not reply to people in haste and not to panic.

If I'm getting moody with Richie and it isn't anything to do with him I'll remove myself from the situation. Perhaps someone sent the wrong work email to someone else, or I've received a nasty comment over Twitter and I'm feeling upset. Richie can't help me with that and I don't want to snap and take it out on him, so I'll get out of the house for a bit. I might go off and walk the dog to calm down or do a workout – exercise really does help.

Since the attack I do have to push myself out of my comfort zone. My inclination now would be to take no risks at all, but you can't live your life that way. I have had to learn to trust and to love again and to take chances, but I do it carefully now, weighing up the odds. I find it harder to do new things and to make connections with new people. But I do it, because I know it's good for me and it's important for Belle and Penelope to see me doing it. I don't want my children to feel tortured by my anxieties. I see Belle dancing around, trusting the whole world and I think, 'That's how I used to be.' I want her to keep that love of life and open heart, but at the same time to be careful and wise.

I also know that if I push myself forward to do something I'm anxious about and it goes well, then I feel good and that helps me manage my future anxiety.

Diane says:

I was always cautious and inclined to be anxious as a young mother, whereas Katie was quite confident from an early age. One afternoon after school she got on the wrong bus home and ended up at the nearby army camp. The school were notified and one of the teachers drove up there to pick her up and brought her back to our house. I had been waiting at the bus stop getting more and more anxious (no mobile phones in those days), until the teacher's car pulled up with Katie in the back seat smiling and waving as if it had been a great adventure. I thought she would be upset and worried, but it didn't faze her at all.

She didn't seem to get very anxious over school either but I don't believe there was the pressure from schools that there is today . . . the national curriculum was in its infancy. There weren't the targets to meet, learning was more fun and it seemed to be within the child's limits. When I finished working in school in 2016, the year two children (aged six to seven) were learning things that years ago were taught in junior school to eight- and nine-year-olds. Nowadays, I don't feel children are given time to consolidate what they have been learning. There seems to be an urgency to go on to the next phase. 'Jack of all trades, master of none' is an old-fashioned phrase but true in today's schools. The pace of learning is very fast and children get anxious if they don't have time to remember what they have learned. I have seen children become very worried about the tests they have to sit, about homework and also about friendships. And this anxiety can often result in behaviour problems, which is something I have also come across at school. They might be unable to concentrate or be tired. Sometimes they get irritable and angry and deliberately cause disturbances in class. Or they will have sudden tummy aches or complain of feeling unwell.

Most schools nowadays have specialist teachers for children with *emotional problems. Years ago, there might have been one or two children in a school with such concerns but the number of children needing extra support has certainly increased. The children I worked with were very young so their anxieties were mainly centred on school or home. Parents splitting up, bereavement, illness of a parent, moving house or moving schools were all issues I came across in school.*

At home, I think talking through a child's fears would be the first step in trying to help. Finding out exactly what is making them anxious, listening carefully and not dismissing their worries as trivial. Empathizing, showing you understand, trying to find practical solutions, instead of just saying, 'Don't worry.' There are books written for children about many topics that cause anxiety and these can be useful for starting a discussion. Professional help is also available both in school and in the community.

Setting the Right Example

It's not surprising that research shows that children whose parents are dealing with intense pressures at work are more likely than their peers to experience similar pressures at school.

Children learn from their parents and the way we conduct our lives as adults often communicates to our children that anxiety is an unavoidable part of leading a successful life. We down caffeine and pack too much into the day, living in a constant state of overdrive and burning ourselves out. And at night, we can end up so wired that we use alcohol and sleep medication to calm down.

Parents can help their children best by setting a good example.

Find ways to slow down, regularly prioritize family time, fun and relaxation, and show your children that life is not just about being driven. Knowing that they will almost certainly do as you do, think hard about how often you are irritable, in a rush or tell them, 'Not now, I'll look at your homework (or painting, or Lego model) later.'

It's also valuable to teach them the coping methods they will need to be more resilient in the face of anxiety-provoking events. While we can't always change the work and life demands that we face, we can change the way we approach them.

The Nervous System

There are two branches of our nervous system that it's useful to know about – the sympathetic nervous system, which is called into action when a 'fight or flight' response is needed, and the parasympathetic nervous system that allows us to rest and digest.

The sympathetic nervous system is the one most of us know best. When we are agitated, rushing, on edge or feeling stressed, it's in full swing as the body prepares for intense activity – muscles tighten, your heart rate increases, blood pressure rises and you begin to sweat. Of course, when fast action is needed, in dangerous or threatening situations, the sympathetic nervous system is vital, it can save life. The problem is that many of us become stuck almost permanently in this mode, on full alert and unable to de-stress, calm down, rest properly or soothe our anxieties.

The parasympathetic nervous system, on the other hand, allows

165

us to rest. When it is activated our blood pressure goes down, our pulse rate slows and our digestive system can function effectively. Muscles relax, our heart rate slows and we conserve energy. In this state we are softer and more accessible.

So how do we access the parasympathetic nervous system? There are lots of techniques that are simple and work well. Meditation, yoga, visualization and deep breathing are all very effective and it's worth finding a way to include a daily practice. The knock-on effects can be surprising – you may well feel calmer and more in control all day. You'll be nice to other people and feel calmer and happier.

Discovering how to access the parasympathetic nervous system is a valuable investment in reducing anxiety and de-stressing. And it's something you can teach your children. Learning a simple, two- or three-minute relaxation exercise, and then teaching it to your children, could benefit the whole family enormously.

RELAXATION EXERCISE

There are a number of simple exercises that help you access a more relaxed state. Here is one you can try with your child.

Sit comfortably in a chair, feet on the floor, hands relaxed in your lap, eyes closed if you would like, although it's fine to keep them open if you prefer. Keep your breathing calm and even.

Now focus on your feet and visualize space inside them. Feel the space as you visualize it, as though your feet were gently expanding like a balloon. Do this for a few seconds and then move your focus up to your lower legs – visualize and feel them filling with space. After twenty seconds or so, move on to your upper legs, and then feel your whole legs filling with space.

Move on to your pelvis, your abdomen and then your lungs, pausing each time to focus on visualizing and feeling space filling each in turn. Go on to your neck, shoulders, arms, hands and fingers. Feel space all the way to your fingertips. And finally visualize your jaw and mouth full of space, and then your whole head, filling with space.

Funny as this may sound, it's easy and it works. As you visualize space in part of your body, that part relaxes its tight muscles and vessels. It's a great exercise to do when you feel as though life has no space and you're overburdened and tense, anxious or stressed.

At times of high pressure, do this several times a day. It can also work well if you do it in bed – it will help you relax into sleep.

How Serious Is Your Child's Anxiety?

Responding to anxiety depends on the individual's sense of control and their capacity to head off or manage the situation that is causing them anxiety and stress. Most of us can manage our own anxiety and can help our children to manage theirs. There is a lot of material online and in bookstores on practical approaches for managing low-level anxiety. However, it is important that parents draw a distinction between low-level and clinical anxiety so that, where anxiety is serious, professional help is sought.

Anxiety is low-level if it's not interfering with the normal day-to-day functioning of your child's life. For low-level worrying and stressing the best things to do as a parent are:

- Be available for talking through problems – but don't focus unnecessarily on the issues.
- Be led by your child's wishes when it comes to further discussion.
- Try to set a good example in terms of getting your own worries into perspective, not over-thinking them or being unnecessarily pessimistic or dramatic.
- Offer practical support – but don't force it.

It's also important to look at your child's routine. Are there too many activities? Too much homework or too great a pressure to do well? Does your child have time to play, to hang about with friends, to do 'nothing much' and to dream? Without this kind of space in her life, she will begin to feel under stress. If necessary, remove some of the activities and some of the pressure. Make sure she knows that the next test, or piece of homework, while it matters, isn't the most important thing in life.

The Danger Zone

When a child's anxiety is such that their symptoms interfere with their ability to sleep or to function in the usual way during the day and appear to be obviously out of proportion with what might normally be expected in any given situation, it is possible that they have the beginnings of an anxiety disorder. There are a number of specific clinically recognized and defined anxiety disorders – for example, generalized anxiety disorder, panic disorder, phobias, social anxiety disorder, obsessive compulsive disorder, post-traumatic stress disorder and separation anxiety disorder. The first port of call should generally be your family's GP who will talk to you about your concerns and, depending upon the age of your child, will talk to her also. The GP will want to ask about:

Difficulties across all parts of the school day and reported difficulties out of school

Changes in core behaviours, such as eating, physical and social activities, sleep, physical care and wellbeing

Social withdrawal, social difficulties

Fears – sudden or unexpected

Concentration difficulties

Developmentally inappropriate behaviours, such as toileting accidents, thumb-sucking, mouthing objects, baby talk, clinginess, temper tantrums

Signs of sadness, being unduly upset, crying easily

Signs of self-destructive behaviour (e.g. head-banging, excessive accidents such as falls or dropping things, and self-harm)

Morbid thoughts and talk (e.g. of injury, death, illness, multiple aches and pains, and catastrophe)

If any of the above 'red flags', which indicate a possible clinical disorder are present, your GP will probably refer you to the local specialist Child and Adolescent Mental Health Services (CAMHS).

They will also give you advice on how to support your child in the short term before they are seen for more in-depth support and treatment over time.

Another route through to getting professional help for your child is to talk to the school's Special Educational Needs and Disability Coordinator (SENDCo). This is useful because it is important to get an idea of how your child is doing at school and also the SENDCo can give you advice or possibly even link with sources of support such as the school's educational psychologist. In some places, CAMHS will actively link with schools and may even provide counselling or clinical psychologist input. Local authority-employed educational psychologists do sometimes work with school staff, setting up projects that target children's mental health and wellbeing. Dealing with stress and anxiety is a topic that is often top of the list because it is so frequently requested by parents and schoolchildren.

Michelle's Story: The Anxious Mother

Michelle's thirteen-year-old daughter Maddie was an active and sociable girl who was doing well at school and was in the football team. Michelle had always been a worrier and she was highly protective of Maddie. She lived in fear of Maddie coming to harm while out and about, travelling to and from school and going to twice-weekly football team sessions, and had always insisted on driving her to and from school and all of her out-of-school activities.

At thirteen, Maddie was aware that this arrangement was a

bit unusual as all of her friends were becoming independent and had started to tease her about her mother's over-involvement. Maddie asked her mum to let her start taking the bus to school. Michelle refused, citing local newspaper items about gangs, muggings and knife-related incidents as her reason for not giving her daughter more freedom. So Maddie began to take matters into her own hands. On several occasions, she left school through a different entrance and walked home with friends. Her mother, beside herself with anxiety, decided to ground her so that she couldn't attend football.

It was only when the football coach, concerned about Maddie's non-attendance, called round and spoke with Michelle that she was able to share her fears. The coach told her that her daughter was one of the most mature and responsible members of the team. Surprised, Michelle realized that she was not seeing Maddie clearly and that she needed to change. She and the coach came to an arrangement in which Maddie and a couple of other girls who lived nearby were allowed to walk together to the pitch. This delighted Maddie, and Michelle – determined not to make Maddie as anxious as she was – went to see a counsellor. Together, they traced her pattern of anxiety back to her own childhood, when her parents divorced and her father disappeared from her life. With support Michelle was able to control her worry over Maddie's safety and, within weeks, Maddie was allowed to travel to and from school with friends as well.

Sarah's Story: The 'Perfect' Child

Sarah was a very well-behaved, obedient child, always keen to win approval. And she did, she regularly won praise from her teachers and parents for her hard work, top marks, good behaviour and maturity. But as Sarah approached her teens she became increasingly anxious, checking and re-checking her appearance in the mirror before leaving the house and going over and over her homework to make sure it was right – spending an hour on a task that was meant to take twenty minutes. She became easily frustrated and angry, and extremely anxious about being embarrassed so that she was reluctant to try new things.

Sarah's mum Annie had always been proud of what a well-behaved and high-achieving daughter she had, but as she noticed the signs of Sarah's anxiety she became concerned. She went to talk to Sarah's teacher, who was concerned that Sarah was being too much of a perfectionist.

The teacher, Sue, explained that perfectionism can be a serious problem: it indicates anxiety in the child and girls are particularly prone to it. Used to being 'good' and receiving a lot of praise, some girls begin to focus too heavily on pleasing adults and winning approval. Instead of being themselves and doing what they enjoy, they feel they must always be doing what others want them to do. Girls with this problem can go on to develop eating disorders and other mental health issues in their teens.

Annie was deeply worried that she might have contributed to the problem and she was keen to find help before Sarah entered her teens. She read up about perfectionism and then, as the two of them were on a relaxed weekend drive to see friends, she talked to Sarah about perfectionism and the damage it can do She explained that she was worried about Sarah and didn't want her to feel things had to be perfect.

Annie explained to Sarah that:

- Everyone fails, messes up and gets things wrong – that's just part of life.
- When things go wrong, you can laugh about it and start again.
- Doing your best is good enough.
- Life is not just black or white, it is full of grey areas.
- She would love Sarah just the same whether she got an A or a D.
- Trying to be perfect is exhausting and doomed to failure!

Over the following weeks, Annie made sure that things were more relaxed at home. She made sure that when she got things wrong herself, she said, 'Oh well, nobody's perfect,' or 'Oops, got that wrong, never mind,' and 'I don't know the answer to that.' And she was careful to praise Sarah for effort, not for results. She looked for opportunities to say, 'You tried hard' or 'That was brave' or simply 'You're pretty special,' rather than 'Wow you got an A.'

Annie also helped Sarah to set a time-limit for home-work and aim to finish it, rather than get it perfect. And she encouraged Sarah to do something new that would be all about having fun. Sarah joined a trampolining club with her best friend and loved it.

And Finally . . .
Remind Them of the Good Things

Children, and adults too, often feel that the world is a terrible place, full of bad news, people being cruel to each other, wars and terrorism. Actually, the world has never been so good, and it's important to acknowledge this ourselves and to tell our children.

By many measures, 2016 was the best year in the history of humanity, with falling global inequality, child mortality roughly half what it had been as recently as 1990, and 300,000 more people gaining access to electricity each day. On average, people throughout the world have been living longer and eating better than ever before. Fewer people die of famine nowadays than in earlier centuries and every measure of material and environmental welfare in the world has improved rather than deteriorated. In fact, the number of people in extreme poverty fell by 137,000 each day for the past twenty-five years.

There's also a bright side to anxiety. Since none of us can avoid it altogether, and some of us are stuck with quite a lot of it, it's worth remembering that it does have some useful functions:

- As humans we need anxiety – it has caused us to avoid dangerous situations. That's maybe why we're still here at all.

- When you're anxious about something you focus on the downside. But the actual event may turn out unexpectedly good – giving you an upside.
- Anxiety produces motivation – it makes us want to get going.
- Anxiety makes you less judgemental of others – you know what it's like to go through a tough time.
- Anxious people make good leaders.
- Anxiety can bring you closer to people – talking it over with someone who knows what it's like creates a bond.
- Anxiety makes you appreciate moments of pure joy.

CHAPTER 10

The Power of No

In the previous chapter, I talked about how many children and young people, girls especially, are suffering from anxiety. And that leads me to the subject of this chapter, because one of the most effective ways to prevent your child from becoming over-anxious is to teach her how to say no.

Saying no carries a thousand meanings – no to being put-upon, no to being a 'pleaser', no to unwanted advances, no to holding back her talent, energy and ideas, and no to trying to be someone other than herself. No is a word that small children learn very young, and it's incredibly powerful.

Saying no means being assertive. And being assertive means being about to stand up for yourself – and for others too – calmly, clearly and with respect for yourself and for everyone else too.

Being assertive is all about refusing to allow your spirit to be crushed. It's about going after what you want in life with determination, but without trampling on anyone else, or turning yourself inside out to get it.

I want my girls to know that they can be strong and nice at the same time. They don't need to steamroller over anyone to get where they want to go, and they don't need to allow themselves to be crushed either. I want them to be able to say no – to me and their dad, to a teacher, to a friend, to a partner and to a boss.

We live in an age when women are achieving so much, and yet so many girls are still being taught to please and placate, to feel 'less than' the men around them, not to make a fuss and to stay silent.

Women in the workplace have ideas and talent but so often they don't put their ideas forward as confidently as the men around them do. 'Good' little girls keep quiet, do as they're told and look after others. Boys, on the other hand, are encouraged to speak up, go for their goals in life and to see themselves as winners.

I believe that children who can be assertive will not only feel better about themselves and be more successful in all the ways that matter, they will be safer too, because they will know how to say no to people who, in any number of ways, want to take advantage of them.

As parents we need to do all we can to make sure our daughters, as well as our sons, grow up confident and able to speak up for themselves and protect themselves. So how do we do this? How do we give them the ability to be assertive when we may not have it ourselves?

What Is Assertiveness?

Assertiveness is a way to communicate feelings, thoughts, opinions and beliefs in a respectful, clear and honest manner. Although it doesn't come naturally to all of us, assertiveness is a skill that can, and should, be taught to children to enable them to stand up for themselves and build resilience.

Assertiveness also builds up their confidence, their self-esteem and their ability to form and maintain stronger relationships.

Assertiveness is very different to aggressiveness. Aggressive behaviour can sometimes be confused with assertive behaviour because both communication styles involve people speaking up for themselves and feeling in control. However, there is a big difference in the way you state your needs in each style. Aggression can be confrontational, rude, bullying and with a hint – or more than a hint – of threat. Aggression puts people's backs up, and it seldom produces positive or cooperative results.

Assertive communication, on the other hand, is direct but not offensive. It is polite and unthreatening. In fact, part of being assertive is respecting others' feelings and opinions, being able to take criticism in a constructive way, and being willing to negotiate when having a disagreement. If you can be assertive you have a huge advantage in life.

Assertive children are more likely to be able to:

Identify their own feelings

Speak up for themselves and others

Avoid and respond to bullying

Make decisions

Disagree respectfully

Negotiate with others

Say 'no' without feeling guilty

Build up stronger relationships

Build confidence and self-esteem

Feel in control

Assertive people are absolutely straightforward in their communications. They don't play games and they know how to level, which means that they don't fall into the three most common behavioural types.

- **The Persecutor:** This is the person who is aggressive, demanding and sometimes rude. This person doesn't listen and tends to throw their weight about. They also think they know best and should be in charge. Their power lies in intimidating others.

- **The Victim:** This is the person who always sees themselves as the victim in any situation, feeling sorry for themselves and wanting others to feel sorry for them. Their power lies in manipulating others through their own 'helplessness'. Of course, there are genuine victims in life, people suffering in all kinds of ways. What I'm talking about here is the person who sees themselves as a victim no matter what else is going on around them.

- **The Rescuer:** This person is always trying to fix things for other people, even when they don't need fixing or could do it for themselves. There are a lot of rescuers about; they tend to fall for victims – anyone who will allow them to be

179

the 'good guy'. The trouble is their 'help' can keep victims feeling negative and helpless. Their power lies in taking charge through an excessive wish to put everything right for everyone else.

Most of us will recognize all three types in the people around us. And it's worth looking at yourself too. We all have a bit of each of these, but for most of us one style is dominant and we use it to try to get what we want in life.

People who know how to be assertive don't need to resort to being persecutors, victims or rescuers. They can be themselves, be clear and honest and direct in a way that doesn't shut the other person down or inflame them. Assertive people are sensitive to other's needs, without compromising their own.

Alice and Olivia's Story

Alice and Olivia had been best friends since they started at secondary school. Two years on, now aged thirteen, the girls walked to school together, met up at break times and often went round to each other's houses at the weekends.

One evening, Alice's mum Liz and dad Brian noticed that Alice was very quiet at supper. After insisting that nothing was wrong, she burst into tears and explained that Olivia was refusing to speak to her.

'Why?' Liz asked her.

'I don't know,' Alice said, wiping away her tears. 'She says I should know what I did. She's been refusing to talk to me for two days. She goes to sit with some other girls at break time and won't speak to me after school. I've begged her loads of times to tell me what I've done wrong but she won't. Now I'm afraid she won't be my friend any more.'

Liz and Brian explained to Alice that Olivia was being unfair. If she had a problem with something Alice had done, she owed it to Alice to explain what it was and try to sort it out.

'She's got you running around after her,' Liz said. 'And it sounds as though she's enjoying having a bit of power.'

'She's done it before,' Alice admitted. 'It's something she does every few weeks and it drives me mad, I just don't know what's wrong and she can keep it up for days.'

'Since begging her isn't working, are you willing to try doing something different?'

Alice agreed and Liz told her to go up to Olivia the next morning and say:

'Olivia, I'm sorry you don't want to speak to me, I'm your friend and I'd like us to sort this out. But if you won't tell me what it's about, then I'm not going to chase after you.'

Liz suggested that, after saying this, Alice carry on her day as normal, chatting and spending time with other girls as though nothing was troubling her.

Alice was unconvinced, but she agreed to try it. Liz pretended to be Olivia so that Alice could practise what she was going to say. After a couple of practices, she said, 'I do feel better, just saying it helps.'

'That's because you're taking back control of the situation,' her dad smiled.

The following day Alice came home from school smiling.

'I did it,' she said. 'I went up to Olivia and said what you told me to say. She ignored me, so I walked away and sat with someone else. Then, at break time, Olivia came up to me and started chatting, as though nothing had happened. She didn't even mention whatever had been wrong.'

'That's great, Alice, well done,' her mum said. 'Not speaking to someone can get pretty boring, you know. I expect Olivia was glad that you gave her an opportunity to stop.'

Finding My Own Assertiveness

Although I was a noisy, friendly, bouncy little girl, I'm not sure that I knew how to be assertive. I was brave – once, aged five, I rode my bike into a brick wall, fell off and got straight back up, onto my bike and rode off. And I was determined to get my way – I could shout and demand when I didn't get what I wanted. Especially in my teens! But despite all of this, I don't think I had any idea of how to be assertive.

Generally, I avoided confrontation, both physical and verbal, and chose to walk away rather than get into a fight. When it came to the freelance modelling world, which was precarious and competitive, I tried always to be pleasant, polite and appreciative. But inevitably girls in that world were often treated badly – made to wait for hours, rejected without explanation, poorly paid and openly criticized. None of it was a confidence boost, but I was young and determined. I kept going and had some successes and I was willing to put up with a lot of poor treatment in the process.

And then I was attacked and my life changed. I woke from the induced coma and realized that someone had tried to control me and silence me through aggression and fear. And I was angry! I thought, 'I'm going to let the whole world know about this. I don't care now because the worst has happened to me, so I will make sure everyone knows what this guy has done to me.'

I became proud of my face as an act of defiance. I decided I would refuse to be embarrassed or hide away. I didn't do anything wrong, why should I live in shame? I think that was when I discovered a new power in myself, the power to stand up for myself and to go out and say what I thought and felt without feeling I had to please, or fear or be controlled by anyone.

The ability to be assertive grew, for me, out of what happened. Even so, I've had to work at it and I've had a lot to learn. When I got to the point of wanting to date again I hit a brick wall, my confidence zeroed – I was shy, afraid of rejection and I wasn't sure how to move forward. But I had learned, by then, that there is always a solution. So I decided to try something completely different and enrolled in an acting class. Going to acting classes when you are lonely or single is a bit of a cliché, but it really did help me. It built my self-esteem and self-worth and taught me a lot about being assertive. Soon after that, I found the courage to go for a coffee with someone and it felt like a big step forward.

I did try dating and I had a couple of rejections from men who took one look at my face and ran a mile. That hurt, but it didn't destroy me. I told myself that they weren't worth worrying about and I got back up. I think that's part of being assertive – knowing your own worth and refusing to let anyone else bring you down.

Now, although I still have more to learn about being assertive, I know that I can stand up for myself and I can say what I think, knowing I matter just as much as anyone else. Communicating is a big part of what I do and when I'm giving a talk I need to have confidence in what I'm saying and in my right to say it.

That's what I want for Belle and Penelope. I want them to be able to speak up for themselves and stand up for themselves. I don't want their choices in life to be limited by their gender or by their fears.

Diane says:

I felt I was treated very differently to my two brothers and I grew up believing boys were better than girls. It didn't help that I was painfully shy, so I easily fitted into the 'placate, give in and not make a fuss' category. Fortunately, as I reached adulthood and my social circle expanded and I moved away from home, I very quickly questioned this and changed my attitude and gradually became more confident and self-assured. As a teacher, I could not condone girls feeling they had to be acquiescent but I do look back in horror at the reading schemes we used in schools in the early 1970s (Ladybird and Through the Rainbow), where the girls and mothers were shown doing domestic work while the boys and dads were mending cars or going fishing. Fortunately, as the years went by and society's attitudes changed so did the books available in schools. Now women and men and girls and boys are shown in an equal light and children show no surprise that dad is cooking while mum mends the car. I certainly tried to bring up all my children to feel equally valued and encouraged them to speak their minds and pursue their interests whatever they may be. It wouldn't have bothered me if my son wanted to do ballet and my girls wanted to play football.

It makes me cross when girls are labelled 'bossy' when they speak their minds. I don't believe boys would be given that label when they speak out. I have seen a great many changes in education in the forty years I have been involved in schools and I believe that nowadays teachers are far more aware of gender equality. Speaking and listening is a big part of the curriculum and both sexes are encouraged to express themselves and be heard. We have to remember to teach our children speaking out doesn't mean being rude or aggressive if it is done in the right way. Self-confidence is one of the most important qualities we can instil in our daughters and we can do that by setting an example . . . not showing our insecurities about our hair, figure, weight, job, friendships etc. We have to praise our daughters for effort as well as success. Our praise has to be less about their appearance and more about their achievements and their personality. Nowadays, there are many more female role models for our daughters: politicians, doctors, athletes etc. They are there in the public eye and have now become the norm. I am not saying our daughters should be pushed into becoming MPs or brain surgeons – it is important to nurture their strengths, they might not be academic, they might not want to go to college or university – but hopefully we can show them all the options and encourage and support them with their choices.

How to Have an Assertive Child

Generally speaking, assertive children grow up to be assertive teenagers and adults. So you can't start too early. It's important to set firm and clear boundaries and to teach them to say no – something I'll return to a bit later. But there are plenty of other things that contribute to teaching your child to be assertive.

Top tips for helping your child to develop assertiveness:

- **Model assertiveness yourself.**

When you speak to your child, or to anyone else in your child's presence, aim to do the following:

- Stay calm.
- Make eye contact.
- Speak clearly and confidently.
- Listen to what the other person has to say.

Remember that your child will do what she sees you do. So act the part, even when you don't feel it.

- **Tell her what assertiveness is.**

You can explain assertiveness to a child by describing different ways of communicating:

- Aggressive people are loud. They might stand too close to you, or try to appear bigger than everyone else. They don't listen to what others say and they are determined to get their own way. In school, an aggressive child who got a bad mark for a piece of homework might be rude to the teacher.
- Passive people use a quiet voice and may not look you in the eye. They often seem unsure of themselves and give in to what others want. In school, a passive child who got a bad mark for their homework might complain about the teacher after class.
- Assertive people look you in the eye and talk calmly and clearly. They know what they want, but they want to hear what you want too and they want everyone to feel OK about the outcome. In school, an assertive child who got a bad mark might ask to speak to the teacher after class to explain that she worked hard on the homework and ask what she could have done differently.

- **Listen to your child and respect what she says.**
This is not the same as giving in to everything she wants. Imagine your four-year-old is having a bit of a meltdown because she wants a snack, but you don't want her to have one as supper is only half an hour away. You can say to her, 'I know you are hungry. Supper is coming soon.' That way she feels heard, but she still doesn't get the snack.

- **Respect your child's privacy.**

Everyone needs some privacy, a room or a space that is their own. Perhaps a box of secrets when they are little, and when they are older, a journal or diary. Never read your child's private writing, or invade their private space. Allow them to feel respected.

- **Let them express emotions.**

Many parents are uncomfortable with certain expressions of feeling – anger, or tears, or sadness. Yet everyone feels these things at times. Don't make the mistake of making your child feel that certain emotions aren't allowed. Teach them, instead, that whatever they feel is OK, whether they are happy or sad, joyful or angry. At the same time, you can teach them to manage their emotions – for instance, by putting the feeling into words, or finding an outlet for it, like drawing a picture.

- **Get them involved in team activities.**

Being part of a team teaches us all kinds of skills – sharing, encouraging others, putting the whole before the individual, learning how to lose, how to cooperate and how to compromise. And most of these skills contribute to learning assertiveness.

- **Encourage decision-making.**

Making choices and decisions is key to learning how to be assertive. In preparation for bigger, tougher decisions later on, give your child choices from an early age. Jelly or ice cream? Tidy toys now or in five minutes? This story or that story before bed? The blue jumper or the yellow jumper?

You can move on, once your child is at school. For instance, let them choose their dish in a cafe or restaurant. They can choose what the family has for supper (and help to make it). They can choose a sport activity for the weekend – football or hockey or tennis.

Later still, your teenager will be choosing which subjects to study, where to apply for a Saturday job, which friends to hang out with, when to say no to a night out.

You'll always be there to guide her choices, but let her make them. And if a choice is something she regrets, or turns out to be wrong (I meant jelly not ice cream! I hate tennis! I wish I'd chosen Art instead of French!), then learning to live with it is also a big part of becoming assertive.

- **Mean what you say.**

Meaning what you say really matters. If you say you'll do something, then do it. Your child needs to see that you will follow through; otherwise what you say doesn't count for much. For instance, if you say no sweets before supper, but she cries and you give her one, she knows that you didn't really mean it and you're easily worn down. Next time she'll keep going with the tears until she gets a sweet. She has sensed your weak spot! How will she ever learn to mean what she says, if she knows that you don't?

Help her to follow through on what she says. For example, if she tells her little brother not to go into her room and take her favourite toy and he does, you can help her to follow this up by talking to her about what she could do. She might put the toy out

189

of reach, ask you to keep it in a cupboard or refuse to play with her brother next time he asks her.

Meaning what you say can't just be for the times when it's easy. It has to hold true for those times when the situation is difficult or someone is upset or disappointed.

Setting Boundaries

Being assertive means being able to set boundaries. If you can do this with your children, they will learn to do it too, for themselves and for others.

A boundary is a limit – a line that cannot be crossed. It might be a simple 'don't touch the glass' or 'stop banging your spoon' or 'no you can't go to the shop on your own'.

Boundaries are not the same as rules. You can't have a rule for everything and that's where boundaries come in; they are often spontaneous and made to fit the situation.

Here are some reasons to set, and keep boundaries:

Being firm with children helps them to feel safe (and in practice often helps to keep them safe, since a lot of boundaries at all ages of childhood and teenage are to do with safety).

Setting boundaries on their behaviour helps them to put the brakes on themselves when they need to. If you stop them from eating a third biscuit, then it helps them learn self-discipline for the future.

Boundaries help children with feelings of uncertainty. A child will be less anxious when they know where you stand – and therefore where they stand.

Boundaries can help teach children to think about others. Otherwise it's all about them and what they want.

Children need boundaries to learn that sometimes they just have to put up with discomfort, annoyance, frustration or having to wait.

You can explain boundaries to a small child by comparing them to a wall or a fence. Point one out to your child and explain that you can't go through them, they're there to keep us in, or out – and safe. A traffic light is another kind of boundary. It's one that we respect because if we cross it there may well be a serious accident.

Physical space is another kind of boundary – one that we can't see but we can all feel. No-one likes to have their space invaded, not even by a hug, unless you're in the right mood for it.

The Value of Saying No

I think no is the most important word I can teach my daughters. Girls are so often taught, by the society we live in, to be 'nice', to placate, to give in and not to make a fuss. But this can lead them into situations that are difficult and even dangerous. There are all kinds of pressures to have sex too young, to take drugs, to expose themselves to things they don't really want and aren't ready to handle. I want Belle and Penelope to be able to say no, to walk away, to be strong, and to kick up a fuss if they need to.

No is setting a firm boundary. It's a significant and emotionally loaded word and it is one we all have to deal with. It's a valuable tool that every assertive girl – and boy – needs to know how to

191

use. Being able to say no at the appropriate time is an important social and emotional skill.

Research conducted at the University of California showed that the more difficulty that you have saying no, the more likely you are to experience stress, burnout and even depression.

And yet saying no is a major challenge for many people.

If this is you, it's worth practising your 'no' a few times. If you know you don't want to do something, then try to avoid, 'Ummm, I'm not sure' or 'I don't think I can make it' or 'I'll look at my diary.' That kind of vague put-off leaves you feeling under pressure to either say yes or try all over again to say no. A simple 'No, I'm afraid I can't do that' leaves you feeling much clearer, and probably relieved.

Saying No to Your Children

When you say no, your children learn to say no. We want our children to walk confidently through life, getting their needs met along the way. Saying no is essential for that. People who can't say no end up feeling overburdened, used by others and resentful. They put their own needs bottom of the list and then feel fed up because no-one else notices. No parent wants that for their child. We want our children to be able to speak up, ask for help and stand up for others.

When you say no to your child it needs to be clear and non-negotiable. Otherwise you say 'maybe' and you can have a discussion about it. A no is usually a question of safety or wellbeing. No to television before homework, or no to video games all evening, or no to staying out late are all, along with a thousand others, about your concern for your child.

It's fine to explain why you said no. But don't let your child make that into a negotiation or a delay.

Here's the kind of conversation I'm thinking of, and how to handle it:

Child: Can I stay up half an hour later? My favourite programme is on.

You: No you can't. Time for bed.

Child: Why not?

You: I'll tell you why not when you're in bed.

Child (whining, one eye on the TV): Tell me why not now.

You (firmly): No. Into bed, then I'll come through and explain why.

You can almost guarantee that once your child is in bed they won't really want to hear the explanation for why they had to go to bed. They know the answer.

Remember also to keep your own boundaries, because our children notice what we do even more than what we say. For example, if you're telling your child, 'no snack before supper,' don't get caught popping a crisp into your mouth.

When Your Child Says No

Even before a child's speech and language skills have begun to develop they can grasp the meaning of no. In developmental terms babies of just a few months can communicate no through gesture and physical movements and in doing so their unique identities and dispositions become evident.

Most parents experience mixed feelings of exasperation and pleasure when their toddlers start to use the word. You're proud of your child for learning the word, and then a little less proud when they're yelling it at you in a shop as you try to drag them out.

It's a delicate line to tread, because children do need to be able to say no, sometimes, and have it respected. For instance, if you ask your child, 'Would you like a kiss?' and she says, 'No,' then you respect this and accept that she's not in the mood. That teaches her a powerful lesson about self-determination. Thankfully, the days of 'Give Auntie Maggie a kiss' are long gone, although you should still insist on politeness.

When No Is a Good Thing

Sometimes it is a very good thing for children and, increasingly, teenagers to say no. Basically, they have to be able to communicate clearly, confidently and assertively that a situation, the way someone else is behaving, in general or to them in particular, or an invitation or a gift is not what they want or need. It may even be harmful to them, we can all think of examples of someone saying yes when it was not in their best interests to do so. A whole campaign for keeping children safe from abuse has centred on the catchphrase 'Say No to Strangers', and this is a core lesson among the many that a child needs to learn. As usual, the example you set of plain-speaking assertiveness rather than aggression or passivity is pivotal. So is your confident non-verbal behaviour.

A child has to learn to say 'not for me' in as confident a way as possible. As a parent, hopefully you can provide a sounding board for them to talk about when they've had to or will have to say no and you can give your perspective from the position of a lot more life experience. You may even need to back your child up if they are saying no in a situation where there is a power imbalance; for example, in a bullying situation where your child is the victim dealing with a group of other children.

When No Is Not a Good Thing

Sometimes, you may need to override your child's no. When your child is being particularly stubborn about a 'no' that just isn't acceptable – for instance, 'no I won't help clear the table' – you can explain to them that, while there are some situations in which they have the right to say no, there are other situations, when they're going against their own interests or the family's interests, where you can overrule them.

There are times when your child is saying no, especially in the teenage years, when things can get very tricky and end up in a standoff. Before you explode, try to view your child's behaviour, however unreasonable or difficult it may seem, as functional. In other words, remember that what they are doing serves some function or need as they see it and this overrides the usually much easier option to behave or conform. As a parent, the better your everyday communication and mutual regard is, the more trust there is in your intent to support their wellbeing and the more chance there is of working things out in a way that suits both you and your child. So aim for mutual respect and potential compromise.

And if all else fails, take a long view of whatever the situation and behaviour is and remember all the times they say yes and behave cooperatively and in a way that you want.

EXERCISE:
NOTICE WHEN THEY SAY YES

Take a little time to think about all the things your child does willingly and says yes to. Try to write three sentences that are about things they have done in the last fortnight that show off their best side. It is important to make your sentences about specific observable behaviours, for example:

She made me a cup of tea when I got home late from work on Monday.
Rather than: She was nice to me when I got home late one night.
She left her room tidy each morning when she went to school.
Rather than: She has been tidy this week.
She took the dog for a walk three times this week.
Rather than: She looked after the dog a bit.

Notice and reinforce the behaviour that you want. For example, if your child goes to bed at a reasonable time, gets a good night's sleep and leaves for school punctually and appropriately organized and equipped, make sure you tell them you've noticed and how highly you rate them for this. All the literature on rewarding and reinforcing 'good' behaviour suggests that rewards are good but should not happen too often, should be relatively unexpected and can take different forms. Sometimes a smile and/or a hug is all that's needed to let them know how well they're doing and as the above example is so much easier for them in terms of how their day will go it will generally be self-reinforcing and will have become so natural they're set up for years to come.

CHAPTER

11

The Guilty Mum (and Finding the Balance)

We've all been there – into a guilt-fest, that is. Why did I do that? I wish I'd done this? Why didn't I know what would happen? Should I have worked or stayed at home? The trouble is giving yourself a hard time for not always getting it right doesn't help. We don't want our children to be consumed by guilt, and that means we have to deal with our own and accept that we aren't always going to make the right choices and sometimes things will go wrong.

In researching this book, I began to wonder why it is that mothers feel so much guilt. Because we do – almost every mother I came across feels guilty about something, mostly small but sometimes large, every single day – and the statistics bear this out, with around ninety per cent of us feeling guilty often. We seem to take responsibility for everything and everyone and then blame ourselves when anything goes wrong.

One study found that, on average, women pend five hours a week – not all of it at once, of course – feeling guilty. But sometimes for mums it can feel more like five hours a day. We feel guilty if we forget the lunchbox, or can't make sports day, or didn't put gloves on her when it's cold, or snapped at her when she threw her food on the floor, or – heaven forbid – did something for ourselves, like sneaking off to an exercise class.

The trouble is the guilt makes us feel bad and it doesn't really help anyone else. It seems to fit along with anxiety in the 'stress' box and to be an inevitable part of life. But is it? Do we have to feel guilty? Or is there something we can do to at least reduce it, even if we can't wipe it out altogether?

Guilt seems to go with having too much to do and not enough hours in the day in which to do it all. That means we have to make choices – play with your daughter or catch up on emails while she's in front of the television, read a bedtime story or grab half an hour for exercise, make a homemade meal or get a takeaway – the list is potentially endless. And it seems that, whatever choice we make, we end up feeling guilty.

I want us time-pressed mums to feel less guilty. So in this chapter I'm looking at why we feel guilt – and what we can do about it.

Being a mother means playing so many different roles at once. As mums we want to be all things to all people, so no wonder it can't always be done. Here's a simple mnemonic to remember just how much it is that we do:

Motivator, esteem builder

Occasional counsellor and rescuer

Teacher and trainer

Homemaker

Ensuring health and safety; nurse and protector

Relationship and life guide and model

Why Do We Feel Guilty?

Given all of the things we do as mothers, perhaps it's not surprising that guilt seems to arrive along with your first child, and from then on it's an almost inevitable part of being a mum. Guilt is what we feel when we blame or condemn ourselves for doing something we perceive to be wrong, or for failing to do something we should have done, or for hurting or harming someone else. Guilt can take many forms, for instance frustration, hopelessness, irritability, poor self-care, even self-punishment, but it is invariably a heavy feeling that affects everyday life, damping down the joys and pleasures.

It doesn't help that we're bombarded with media images of perfect mums, or stories about mothers who've damaged their children, even before they're born, by eating runny cheese, or being depressed, or being too active, or not active enough and so on. From the start, there's so much to be aware of and look out for and avoid and do right that it feels impossible. But to get it all perfect is just not possible.

The biggest portion of guilt seems to stem from not being able to do it all. And we can't. We want to be good mothers and we want, or need, to go out to work. We want to run the home and we also want time to be ourselves.

And there's lots of pressure piled on – by our own mothers, by the media, by the stay-at-home versus out-to-work mum groups in the playground, and most of all by us, telling ourselves we failed.

The trouble with guilt is that it makes us miserable. It nags away in our heads, going on and on about what we should have done and replaying our moments of 'failure' over and over again. And it's not as though feeling guilty does much good – studies prove that it can affect our concentration and therefore efficiency and productivity.

So, what is it that we feel guilty about? Here's a list of the things most mothers say trigger guilt:

- Going out to work
- Saying 'in a minute' when children want our attention (and then not being available a minute, or even ten minutes, later)
- Not spending 'quality' time with the children
- Losing our temper
- Going out and having fun
- Giving more than one child equal time and attention
- Letting children watch too much television
- Neglecting partners
- Neglecting ourselves

The list could go on and on, we've all got our particular issues and triggers. It's worth writing your own list, just to get clear about the things that do regularly nag at you. Think also about the impact guilt has on your life. It may affect your moods, your energy, your ability to work and to get things done and your enjoyment of time with your children or friends and family.

The Positive Side of Guilt

While constant guilt can wear us down and does no good at all, there is an aspect of guilt that can serve a function. Sometimes guilt alerts us to a wrong choice. Guilt can be the voice that tells you you're not living life in the way that you would like. If there's a constant nagging sense of guilt about one issue, as opposed to the myriad everyday things, then ask yourself if there is a purpose to your guilty feelings. Sometimes guilt can be what motivates us to make changes that make life better. Guilt is one of those negative emotions that can let us know we've got something we need to learn, or change or do differently.

For instance, I had a friend who felt constantly guilty and miserable about not spending any time with her husband. Children and work came first and her husband was a neglected third. She decided to do something about it and she started to put aside time just to be with him. It wasn't easy, and it wasn't much (just a couple of hours a week), but he noticed and appreciated it and things became warmer between them. Her guilt had been helpful. Guilt isn't always a pointless emotion – it can be good for you if it leads you to bring about a positive change. It can alert us to something, or someone, that we need to pay attention to. So, take a look at what you feel guilty about – is there something that you need to do, or to change?

My Guilty Feelings

There are loads of things I've felt guilty about as a mum. I've always worked, I need to and I also love my work. But in the early days I sometimes felt miserable – I felt I was missing out on time with Belle when she was very small and that hurt. It was hard thinking that other people were seeing some of the special moments in her life when I wasn't. And, of course, I am not alone; around two-thirds of mothers with children under eighteen work. And I know that a lot of them, like me, feel guilty.

It took me a while to understand that one of the best things I could do for Belle and Penelope was to show them that you can be a good mum and a working woman, the two can and should fit together. Life is all about balance, and although this can be a tough balance to find, it is possible to do both without feeling guilty.

For me, time with Belle and Penelope will always be precious, but time at work is valuable too. Work gives me a sense of self and accomplishment and fulfilment that is very different from the joy I get from my girls. And I've finally realized it's OK to have both. Life is about fitting in the people and things you love and finding a way to bring it all together. I can't say that I never feel guilty about this particular issue – I do. But I've made my peace with it now. I come in from work and put it aside to spend time with the girls and that's something I look forward to every day.

I've made the decision to be as good a role model as I can for my daughters, and that means keeping my guilty feelings in check and showing them the many benefits of being lucky enough to have work I love and a family I love too.

I've always kept a journal. I don't write in it every day, but only when I need to. It helps me to make sense of things that have happened, to sort out what I feel and what I want to do and to let off steam when I need to.

Diane says:

I think mothers are programmed to feel guilty! From my teacher training I knew how important parental support and involvement was in a child's life, so I always tried to be there for my children, playing with them, organizing activities, doing homework and so on. Motherhood seemed extremely child-centred and if you didn't get it right you were made to believe your child would be damaged for life!

Yes, I did feel guilty, there is always that feeling that you're not good enough. I felt that, since it was my choice to have children, I had to do the job properly. In the early days, when I just had one child I wanted to be super-mum, with a tidy house, wholesome food on the table and clean clothes in the drawers. I felt I had to justify being at home all day and would feel bad when things didn't run smoothly. After babies number two and three, it wasn't so easy and then more guilt crept in; not spending enough time with each child, trying to find activities suitable for all ages, being irritable with the older ones because the baby kept you awake at night, not getting any housework or shopping done. I used to remind myself of a phrase I had read somewhere, 'Your children won't remember if they had a tidy house but they will remember if you spent time with them,' so I was able to stifle those guilty feelings because I believed rightly or wrongly that I was doing the best for my family.

When something goes wrong in a child's life, then guilt kicks in again. Was it my fault? Have I brought them up badly, have I done too much or not enough? Am I a bad parent? This was to a certain extent how we felt when Katie was attacked – we blamed ourselves. All sorts of things went through our minds: we didn't equip her for the harsh realities of life, we should have been stricter with her, we should have talked to her about the choices she was making and on and on. Logically, we know we shouldn't blame ourselves, what happened was a one in a million thing and absolutely not our fault or Katie's, but guilt is a difficult feeling to cope with and it takes a lot of thought and rational discussion to work through it.

So, what is the answer for mothers feeling guilty? First, recognizing that these feelings come from wanting to be the best parent possible, but also accepting that no-one is perfect. Try to be confident in the choices you have made and understand why you made them. All children are different and so are parenting styles and mothers should celebrate what they are doing well and look at what they have, not what they think they are missing out on. Don't compare yourself unfavourably to other parents as their life choices will have been made for different reasons, but sharing your experiences and knowing that you're not the only mum feeling guilty over certain things can be very reassuring and can help keep things in perspective. I know there are many parenting forums available online nowadays where parents can let off steam or ask for advice and in an anonymous setting it is probably easier to admit to needing support without feeling judged. It can be reassuring to know others feel the same way.

EXERCISE:
WORKING ON YOUR OWN GUILT

If you are always feeling weighed down with guilt, then you need to be your own psychologist in a way. The starting point for addressing issues of this nature is to analyse and try to make sense of how it is affecting you and your life:

- Try asking yourself what is contributing to your guilt? What exactly are you being critical about? How are you not living up to your own expectations? What is contributing to this, such as financial, emotional or social issues?
- Take stock and carry out a kind of audit of your personal resources and debits, such as achievements, existing commitments, material, personal and social weaknesses and strengths.
- Brainstorm possible ways forward and creative solutions: What resources are immediately available and what can I work towards getting? Where can I get support? What can I manage without?

Dealing with Guilt

We all feel guilty from time to time, but if you feel that guilt is a serious issue in your life and is affecting your happiness and relationships, then it's time to take a look at what is going on. With a little time and effort, there's a lot you can do to understand and reduce your sense of guilt.

Be a Good Enough Mother

The phrase 'good enough mother' was first coined by paediatrician and psychoanalyst Donald Winnicott back in 1953. Today, we use it a lot, but what does it mean?

Winnicott spent a lot of time watching mothers with young children and he realized that babies and children actually benefited when their mothers failed them in what he called 'manageable' ways.

If we try to be perfect parents, then we are setting our children up to feel that they have to be perfect. If we make mistakes, fail sometimes, get things wrong, then they can too. And if we deal with those imperfections and show that they are not the end of the world, we give our children the gift of knowing that they can fail, or get something wrong and it's not the end of the world.

It's much easier to let go of guilt in this context. If we know it's alright not to be perfect and to get things wrong, then we needn't feel guilty. We can sort it out, put it right or laugh it off and carry on. And we can respond to a twinge of guilt a bit like an alarm buzzer. Do I need to respond to this – or switch it off? If I can put it right or do something positive, I'll respond. If not, then guilt won't help. Time to switch off the nagging 'not good enough' voice.

It helps to keep things in perspective through:

- Discussion with others – other mothers, relatives and friends
- Conversation online through websites and forums like Mumsnet
- Reading magazines and literature about motherhood

Here are a few examples of unhelpful ways of talking to yourself that may be supporting your guilty feelings.

All or Nothing Thinking

Do you tend to think in broad generalizations, such as 'I never get it right as a mother', 'I always overreact when my child is naughty' and so on. When you do this, you can start to feel pretty hopeless, because you're condemning yourself to never getting it right. To help you stop this, try to take each incident on its own. If you think, 'I've overreacted today, but I don't always and I can choose not to next time', then you can keep it in perspective and see that actually nothing is always or never, most things are in the middle and you can choose to make next time different.

Black and White Thinking

This is where you decided that something, or someone, is either one extreme or the other and the two will never meet. And you tend to put yourself at the negative end of the spectrum. For instance, 'My friend Mary is the perfect mother and I'm no good as a mother.' Or 'Annie is never tired after work and I always am.' These statements simply aren't true. Mary is not perfect, and Annie does get tired. Try to see things as they are, in all the shades of grey that come between black and white.

Perfectionist Thinking

With this way of thinking, you tell yourself that if you don't get everything perfect you'll be seen as hopeless. For example, 'I didn't take my child to school on time last Friday so the school will think

I am totally disorganized.' Or 'I can't let my child leave the house without fresh, clean clothes or I'll be a neglectful mother.' You won't, you'll just be like every other mother – occasionally you're late, sometimes the children have clean clothes and sometimes they don't. Most of the time no-one minds, or notices, except you. You are your own toughest judge.

Here are some other useful things you can do to help keep guilt at bay:

- Keep a journal, highlight the positives and turn the things that didn't go so well into points for development and growth.
- Remember the example you are setting for your child in terms of positivity, optimism and self-regard.
- Remember that you are the example of how it is to live life, with its challenges, its opportunities for learning and its opportunities for finding solutions.
- Be aware that for every mother there will be unique challenges, which come complete with failures and successes.
- Adopt a 'cup half full' rather than half-empty mindset.
- Be in the moment as much as possible.
- Remember that you know more than you think you do. This was first coined by the famous parenting specialist Dr Spock. Trust your gut, that unique knowledge you have built up over time and your own hard-won expertise.
- Focus on the things you do really well and feed your confidence.

C-O-N-F-I-D-E-N-C-E

To help banish guilt, think about confidence – how much you have and how much you already do well. And use this simple mnemonic to increase your confidence when it's at a low ebb:

Can-do mindset – think of all your previous achievements

Only you have knowledge of your unique situation

No-one is judging you more than yourself

Friends can help with boosting your parenting self-esteem. Make it a mutual process

Individual situation, resources, strengths and weaknesses – be aware of all these

Decide what your priorities are and then base what you do as a parent around these

Enjoy the everyday pleasures, joys and challenges

Nobody can parent from a rule book – you have to engage and learn and find solutions daily

Care but don't constrict – as children get older your job is to gradually let go while keeping them safe and being their safety net and sounding board

Ensure communication lines are always kept open

And Finally – Remember the Oxygen Mask!

During the safety demonstrations on aeroplanes the cabin crew tell you that, in the event of oxygen being necessary, first fit your own oxygen mask before you attend to your children and babies. That's because, if you haven't looked after yourself, you can't look after anyone else. It's a useful thing to remember in life. If you become exhausted, burn out or go under, then everyone in the home will suffer. Mothers are at the heart of a family and, without them, families suffer. Looking after yourself, giving yourself some care and tenderness, space and time is not selfish and not something to feel guilty about. It's a necessity.

Meryl and Hayley's Story

Meryl became a new mum when she was only nineteen, barely more than a child herself. Her daughter, Hayley, arrived two months early and spent her first few weeks of life in a special baby care unit incubator. From the start, Meryl was extremely protective of Hayley who was a little behind developmentally and very dependent upon her. Meryl was afraid that Hayley's early birth was in some way her fault, something that she had done, although she had no idea what. She felt deeply guilty and she tried in every way she could to make this up to Hayley by being the best possible mother. But, in trying to be perfect, Meryl always fell short of her own expectations. She tried never to be angry with Hayley, always to dress her in lovely clothes, to put her first in everything and to make sure she never suffered in any way. She kept Hayley very sheltered from other people, afraid that her little daughter was extra-vulnerable and might become ill.

Meryl's mother Tansy tried to point out that Meryl was in fact smothering Hayley by over-protecting her and trying to make everything perfect. She knew that Meryl felt guilty and tried to tell her that, as doctors had confirmed, Hayley's early arrival was not her fault, it was just one of those things that can happen. But Meryl didn't listen. She devoted herself to Hayley and refused ever to go on a date or to let anyone else into their small world.

When Hayley reached her teens, she began to rebel. She found a group of friends at secondary school and began staying out after school with them. Then she began sneaking out to go to parties. Meryl was beside herself – suddenly she couldn't control Hayley as she always had. She lost her temper, shouting at Hayley, 'I've done everything for you, given up everything for you and this is how you thank me.'

Hayley looked at her mum. 'I didn't ask you to do that, Mum. You always felt guilty about me, but you didn't need to, I'm fine. And I don't want to be fussed over or wrapped in cotton wool. I want to go out and have a good time and have friends and live my own life.'

Meryl was shocked. That evening, she thought for a long time, and she realized that her guilt had been affecting all her actions, and it had affected Hayley too.

Meryl went to see a counsellor, who helped her to see that Hayley's early birth was not her fault. And gradually Meryl began to deal with her own feelings of guilt and to accept that Hayley needed the freedom to grow up and make her own mistakes.

It wasn't easy for Meryl to step back and let Hayley go. But one day her mum, Tansy, hugged her and said, 'I thought you'd never stop feeling guilty about Hayley's birth. It was as though you felt everything had to be perfect after that. But you've changed, you're letting Hayley have a life. I'm proud of you.'

CHAPTER 12

The Teenage Years

The teenage years are a hugely important time. They can also be a turbulent, uncertain and testing time – for the teenager and for her parents too. The years from age thirteen to nineteen are when a child makes the transition to being a young adult. Along the way, their body matures rapidly, they have growth and hormone spurts and sometimes what they do doesn't make sense to them, let alone anyone around them.

As long as we've had teenagers, they've had a bad press and this major period of development – cognitive, physical, sexual, emotional and social – is commonly characterized by inner turmoil and difficult behaviour. In practice, this can mean a gregarious child who suddenly wants her life to be 'private' from her mum, a bright child who wants to leave school because it's 'boring', a child who suddenly stops eating (or eats too much), a previously sensible child who suddenly takes huge risks, or a happy child who becomes moody and even depressed.

For parents it's a minefield. We can be coasting along, thinking we're doing a pretty reasonable job, when suddenly our little girl becomes a teenager and we're living with a stranger. And one we're not sure we like very much.

At this point, it helps to look back and remember our own teenage years, which were almost certainly none too perfect. We came through, and our children will too, with a bit of support and guidance. Our teenagers are pulling away from us, they want – and need – to be independent and we need to encourage this. But they also need us to keep loving and believing in them, even though at times it feels as though we're just there for them to rebel against.

I do feel a bit nervous when I think of my girls reaching their teens, because I wasn't exactly a perfect teenager myself. I gave my parents plenty of headaches, and I'm probably in for a few myself. But I do remind myself that teenagers aren't monsters. They may take a bit of understanding and patience, but underneath all the uncertainty and peer pressure they're still the kind, funny, loving children we adore. And they'll become adults we also adore. So it's worth navigating the bumpy teenage years with tenderness and care.

Teenage Changes

The teenage years are definitely a time of change. And these changes can be summed up by two processes going on in your budding teenager – puberty and adolescence.

215

The term puberty sums up the physical changes that a child's body goes through in order to become a fully sexually mature adult, capable of having children of her own.

In reality, puberty can begin in some children as early as eight, and many of the key changes have happened by the age of fifteen.

It's vital that you prepare your child for puberty. By the age of eight, every girl and boy should know the changes that they will go through and how to manage them. As well as letting them know that you're available to talk, you need to sit them down and explain, in clear and simple terms, what they can expect.

For girls, the external changes are breast development and periods and extra (in particular genital and underarm) body hair. For boys, the changes are a larger penis and testicles, a deepening of the voice, and body hair on genitals, underarm, chest and face. At the same time, both girls and boys have growth spurts and their bodies grow and fill out.

On average, girls begin this process at age ten to eleven, and boys around eleven to twelve. As parents, you need to make the conversation practical. Girls want to know when they will need (or get) a bra and how to manage periods. A lot of girls worry a huge amount about when their first period will start and how they'll manage it. One friend told me her daughter felt a whole lot better when she read a leaflet advising that, if you've got nothing else to hand, take a sock off and use that. But most girls begin to carry sanitary items in their schoolbags once it's clear that puberty is beginning.

While the physical signs are evident, your children need to know that all kinds of other changes are happening under the surface.

These changes come under the umbrella of adolescence. As the physical changes happen, hormones are in overdrive and this affects behaviour and feelings. That's why some children announce the onset of adolescence with fairly dramatic changes in behaviour. They can become easily distracted, thoughtless, rude or withdrawn.

They take more risks and care passionately about their friends, while apparently caring very little for anything you have to say.

At this stage, teenagers are starting to pull away from their parents or carers, forging a path towards living independently as adults. They have to make choices and decisions and to find their identity and place in the world – and that can feel like a very tall order.

At this time, teenagers are forming their own views about life and the world around them. Frustrated because they're still treated like children, but at the same time often a bit daunted by the prospect of independence, they literally fall between the planks, and they can feel very adrift.

Our job, as parents, is to keep things stable, to manage our own feelings and not to overreact when our darling children suddenly appear down the stairs with dyed black hair, torn T-shirts and nose-rings, or with pelmet-high skirts, teetering heels and six coats of eye-liner.

Take a deep breath and remember – it will pass!

T-E-E-N-A-G-E-R

What is a teenager? This mnemonic is a good way of thinking about the answer to that question:

Tester – someone who is pushing the boundaries and finding their own way

Energetic, active and dynamic

Emotional – with strong and changeable moods

Normal – most teenage behaviour is normal. And normal is what they want to be

Angry – at times, as well as dogmatic and stubborn

Gregarious – teenagers are usually sociable

Egoistic – most teenagers are very self-focused

Risk-taker, innovator, creative outside-the-box thinker

Seeker – of enjoyment, excitement, new experiences

My Teenage Years

I'm going to own up right from the start – I was a difficult teenager.

I think I was fine until I reached secondary school. But at that point I smelled the heady scent of freedom. I began to go around with some kids who my parents thought weren't the greatest influence but, to be honest, I wasn't being swept along, I was more of a leader and instigator.

By the time I was fifteen, I wanted to go out and I wasn't about to let anyone stop me. I think my poor parents felt as though they'd been hit by a hurricane. My older brother hadn't caused them any problems – he was quiet and academic and happy as long as he had a computer. But in my case, it was all slamming doors and shouting. Phrases like, 'It's my life, I can do what I want,' 'You can't stop me,' and 'It's none of your business' from my side, and 'You're grounded' from Dad's.

I wanted to be a rebel; smoking, drinking, going to parties, dressing up and having fun. There was always a part of me looking for excitement and pushing the boundaries. I couldn't wait to go out and lead my own life. That was probably because my home life had been so stable and secure, I felt very sure of my parents. I knew they'd always be there, so in a funny way it was safe to push them away.

I wanted glamour and excitement and I dreamed of the modelling and TV world. I don't think my parents thought much of that, and they had a point – no real future, no consistent income or security. But, of course, as a teenager that didn't matter to me, all I could see was the bright lights, drawing me like a magnet.

I'd be mortified if Belle and Penelope did what I did and I'm well aware that they probably will! I just hope that Richie and I can provide the same secure base for them that I had. No matter how many battles we had, my parents were always consistent in their love and support and, looking back, I am so grateful to them for that.

Funnily enough, I never shout these days. I hate raised voices and arguments, I prefer things nice and peaceful and I'm hoping we can keep it that way as the girls hit their teens.

Diane says:

I always felt confident as a mum in the primary school years. I enjoyed doing arts and crafts, cooking, reading to the children and playing games, and David would let them help in the garden with various things. But it was a different story when they were in secondary school. Katie enjoyed the social side of school more than the academic and we had many battles about homework, uniform, hair styles, make-up and so on. She always liked to push the boundaries just to see what she could get away with and I think as parents we were out of our comfort zone. Thank goodness I had David to back me up when I nagged her! She'd go to school with no make-up on and arrive home with it on and I'd look at her and think, 'Hang on, you didn't go out this morning looking like that.'

I caught her in town having a crafty cigarette. She must have been fifteen and she was leaning against a wall with her friend. I stormed over and said, 'What on earth are you doing?' And she looked at me calmly and said, 'Having a fag'. That was her attitude – you can see what I'm doing, what a silly question.

The teen years, especially from sixteen to nineteen, were definitely the most challenging in my relationship with Katie. At that stage you feel control over their lives slipping away and realize that you have to pick your battles. We'd say, 'Do this . . .' and she'd do the opposite. She was very good at getting around us – she'd say, 'You trust me, don't you?' and we'd say, 'Of course,' and then she'd say, 'Well then, I'll be back later and I'll be fine,' and off she'd go.

She would play us off against each other too. I'd say no to a new dress and she'd go to her dad, who was much more of a soft touch. He'd had a very tough childhood himself, so he loved being able to give our children things. He'd drive her to the shop and then sit outside while she bought the dress!

We couldn't always persuade her to be sensible or fix things for her. You have to let them make their own mistakes, as long as they learn from them and they are not mistakes that have dire consequences. It's on the big decisions that you have to put your input as they don't have enough knowledge to make the decisions. For instance, leaving home. Katie was determined to move out when she was nineteen, and it wasn't sensible since she was a trainee beautician and would barely be earning enough to live on. We decided that if we couldn't stop her we had better help her, so we paid the deposit on her room, bought things she needed and slipped her petrol money every now and then.

Looking back, I wish I had talked more to Katie and my other children about the pitfalls in life and how to navigate them. I didn't find that side of things easy. And, of course, there was so much that they were experiencing, with the dawning age of technology, that I knew very little about.

I worried a lot about Katie as a teenager, far more than I needed to because actually she was hard-working and determined and she forged her own path, and I was proud of her for that.

The bottom line is that parenting is an inexact science! No-one knows the right way, we all get it wrong sometimes. All we can do is to love our children and do our best.

The Teenage Brain

Teenagers do seem to do some pretty baffling things at times. And some crazy ones. And some that just don't make sense. But there is a reason – it all comes down to the teenage brain, which is still very much in development. Their bodies might look pretty adult at fifteen or sixteen, but their brains are not at all the same as the adult brain. Research has now shown that the brain takes far longer to form completely than was previously thought. And that results in several behaviours that parents need to understand.

Risk-taking

This is top of the list because it's potentially so worrying. Why do they do it? Teenagers often hurl themselves into all kinds of things that would make any sane adult think twice. Like careering around in an old banger with six other teenagers and a drunk newly qualified seventeen-year-old at the wheel. Or going surfing in a storm. Or running right up to the edge of a cliff. Or downing so much alcohol that they can't remember where they live, let alone the way home. Or trying drugs because, well, everyone does and it's cool and what can really go wrong?

We tend to say, in exasperation, 'Why didn't you just think?' But in teenagers, the frontal lobe (where our decision-making happens) is not as connected to the rest of the brain as it is later in life. Making them more likely to take risks and less likely to think it over.

On the plus side, they may also be willing to take more positive risks too, like auditioning for the school play, standing up to give a speech or asking someone on a date.

Giving in to Peer Pressure

The other thing that influences teenagers is peer pressure. Add that into the mix and teenage risk-taking soars to scary levels.

Teenagers care what their friends think far, far more than they care what their parents think. Where once you were all-seeing and all-knowing to your adoring children, now they're more likely to dismiss your opinion in a millisecond in favour of what their friends think. Suddenly you're in the 'old and boring' category, and it can hurt.

One study using MRI scans on adults and teenagers showed that their brains reacted very differently to the presence of friends when making a decision. It found that teenagers who would not take risks when alone or with an adult were far more likely to take risks when their friends were watching. The reward centre of the teenage brain became much more active in the company of their peers. In adults, however, the reward centre's activity remained at a constant level no matter who was watching.

Peer pressure in teenagers is huge. They want to be part of the crowd and to fit in and that means doing what the others do. If your teenager has reasonably sensible friends, that's alright, you can live with being told you know nothing. But if their friends are trouble, then you may have to step in to keep your child safe.

Appearing Uncaring

It can sometimes seem as though teenagers don't care what others are feeling. They can be insensitive and appear uncaring. But studies have found that teenagers have a much harder time correctly interpreting vocal inflection and facial expressions. They judge expression using a totally different part of their brain from the part which adults use. Teenagers use a part of the brain called the amygdala, which largely controls emotions, while adults use the part of the brain controlling logic and reason.

As a result, teenagers often get it wrong. When they are shown pictures of people in various emotional states – sadness, fear, consternation and disappointment – teenagers interpret them, at least half the time, as anger. This means that your teenager may think you're angry with them even when you're not. And they may seem uncaring because they're not responding accurately to someone else's feelings. If they are seeing anger when in fact there is sadness on someone's face, they will respond in what seems to us an inappropriate way, but seems to them perfectly normal.

Having Trouble Concentrating

Teenage brains are still pretty chaotic. In fact, they are more like the brain of a small child than an adult, even as their body begins to appear more adult. Scientists looking at teenage brains found a lot of activity in the frontal lobe – far more than would occur in an adult. The teenage brain is trying to take in and process everything going on around it and it becomes easily overloaded, making it difficult for them to concentrate.

The adult brain works far more efficiently, making it easier to concentrate.

It's also worth noting that IQ, the measure of intelligence, can fluctuate a great deal during adolescence. Which explains why a child who was getting As suddenly gets Ds. The teenage brain is evolving, reshaping and streamlining itself, and in the process all kinds of weird and wonderful things can happen.

All of this means that we parents have to go gently and carefully with our teenagers. They may think they know everything and understand the world, but they honestly don't, and even if they think they don't need us, they do – in some ways more than ever.

Parenting a Teenager

Being a parent to a teenager isn't as alarming as it can appear from all you read and hear. Because, despite those lurid stories of out-of-control teenagers, most of them are pretty normal and they want to get on with everyone around them, including you.

The rebellious, wild teenager continually at odds with mum and dad is one of the common stereotypes of adolescence. But, although this may be the case for some kids and it is certainly *is* a time of emotional ups and downs, that stereotype is absolutely *not* representative of most teens.

The major challenge for most teenagers is that of seeking their own identity, which means putting some psychological distance between themselves and their parents, although their need for the security and wisdom of loving parents is just as great as when they were younger. In an ideal world, the parents of teenagers would deal with their own frustrations and confusion and at the same time have all the answers and skills needed for ensuring their child's high self-esteem and confidence. Parents also need to support their child with a whole range of issues, such as:

- Education
- Relationships and sex education, including emerging sexuality and contraception
- Personal issues such as confidence and body image
- Social issues such as shyness and bullying
- Drugs, alcohol or substance use
- Money and personal finances

As for all human relationships, the foundation for being a good parent is communication, and to have that you need to be sensitive to when your teenager needs to talk and be available. Sometimes, they may just need to 'sound off' and all they need is for you to listen and be understanding. Other times, they may need information or practical support. The only way to be clear about what they need is to listen and this means that all of your own experience and the answers that you worked out when you were growing up don't necessarily get voiced straight away and maybe don't get voiced at all. The behaviour and the issues that your teenager is experiencing are intrinsic to the world in which *they* are growing up in and, in many ways, they are better informed about that than you. The only way to start to help in an effective way is to let them tell you about their experiences and issues and ask you their own questions, so that you can help them find the answers.

As teenagers mature, they start to form their own ideas, beliefs and moral code, and parents may find that children who had previously been willing to conform to please them, suddenly begin asserting themselves and their opinions more strongly and rebelling against parental control.

This is a good thing. A teenager who simply goes along with what her parents want may be facing more future problems than one who puts up a fight over certain issues or who demonstrates her independence and her own style and opinion, even if that leads to conflict.

It's worth looking closely at how much room you give her to be an individual. Ask yourself questions such as: Am I a controlling parent? Do I listen to my child? Do I respect my teenager's opinions and choices?

Mattie and Cara's Story

By the time Cara reached the age of fifteen, her mum, Mattie, felt that she was living with a stranger. Cara had always been a well-behaved, easy child, full of fun and very close to her mum, dad and younger brother. So Mattie thought the teenage years would be straightforward. But by the time Cara was fifteen, war was raging in their home. Mattie, a hotel manager, disapproved of just about everything Cara was doing, wearing and saying. Her skirts were too short, her make-up too heavy, her music too loud, her schoolwork not good enough and her friends not suitable. Cara, on the other hand, thought her mum was bossy, domineering, old fashioned, out of touch and only interested in her own opinion.

Cara's dad, Pete, did his best to rein them both in and get everyone talking, while her little brother Dom just hid from the rows. But nothing seemed to stop the conflict. And the more Cara and Mattie rowed, the more miserable everyone in the house became.

One lunchtime at work Mattie complained about Cara to her friend Zoe. 'She's a nightmare,' Mattie moaned. 'Why can't she just do as she's told?'

'She sounds pretty normal to me,' Zoe said. 'I've had two teenage daughters and it wasn't easy. Teenagers need to start doing their own thing, at least in some ways. Are you sure you're not being a bit hard on her?'

Mattie was startled. She had expected Zoe to be on her side, not Cara's.

'I'm on both your sides,' Zoe said. 'You both want peace, don't you? Tell me what your teenage years were like?'

Mattie admitted that her own mother had been very hard on her. She'd had strict rules and tough consequences if she broke them. 'Actually, I was pretty unhappy,' she admitted. 'I felt my mum didn't give me any freedom at all and I was furious with her. I couldn't wait to leave home.'

'And yet it seems as though you're using her as your model in dealing with Cara,' Zoe said. 'It might be time to be a bit softer, talk a bit more, reach a few compromises. We know a lot more about teenagers these days, they're trying to prepare themselves to manage without us, and we need to help them.'

Zoe told Mattie about the My Teenage Wish List Exercise (over) and suggested she do it for herself that evening. Mattie did, and what she remembered about her own teenage wishes made her stop and think. Her own mother hadn't supported her need for independence at all. Perhaps she was being a bit hard on Cara.

That weekend, Mattie asked Cara to help her decorate an old chest of drawers. Cara was reluctant, but she had always enjoyed arts and crafts and she was amazed when Mattie said she could choose the colours and design.

As they worked together, Mattie talked to Cara. She explained that she realized she was being a bit heavy-handed and that Cara needed some freedom. She asked Cara some of the questions (from the exercise) that she would have liked her mother to ask her. Cara, wary at first, began to open up and to tell her mother what really mattered to her. She loved clothes and make-up and wanted to go into fashion design. Mattie said she would support that, and agreed to be less critical of Cara's choices of make-up and clothes. In return, Cara said she would work harder at school and agree and stick to curfew hours.

It was a start, and over the following weeks there were noticeably fewer rows and more talking and laughter in their home. Mattie began to appreciate Cara's very original fashion choices (and to ignore her very heavy painted-on eyebrows and inch-thick foundation) and Cara stuck (mostly) to her promise to come in on time after a night at a friend's and to work harder in school.

EXERCISE:
MY TEENAGE WISH LIST

Here's the exercise that Mattie did. It takes us back to our own teenage years in an effort to understand what our child is going through as a teenager.

Think back to the most challenging part of your own teenage years and write a wish list for what you would have liked at that time.

Mattie's example:

Underlying need	What I needed	The questions I would like to have been asked
1. To be myself (identity)	Encouragement Praise for the good things I did	What do you enjoy doing most?
2. To have the relationships that I want	Space and freedom to develop friendships and relationships of my own, and guidance and support when I asked for it	What makes a good friend/relationship? How can you look after yourself and make good relationship choices?
3. To be independent	Support and encouragement to make my own decisions and to take more responsibility for my life	How would you like to become more independent and is there any help you need to do so?
4. To have goals and ambitions	Information and help with gaining everyday life skills such as cooking, managing money, health and education and work plans	What do you want to do in life? What do you need to learn? What information do you need?

Parental Strategies

Parenting a teenager takes a thoughtful, self-disciplined approach. Doing it successfully involves keeping a cool head – and several strategies at once:

Monitor them.

Keep them busy.

Keep talking.

Deal with conflict.

Balance rules and negotiation.

Monitor Them

This is vital. You need to know where your teenager is and what they are doing and there's no compromise on this, because you need to know they are safe. If your teenager tries the 'Don't you trust me?' line (as I did!) then don't fall for it. Say something along the lines of, 'It's not about you, it's me – I need to know that you're safe. So humour me.'

Keep Them Busy

By this I mean that a teenager who has out-of-school interests, such as sport, drama, art, music and so on, is far less likely to get up to no good (involved in drink and drugs) and is also less likely to be angry, depressed and anxious. These activities give life purpose, they bring rewards, including self-esteem, and they provide motivation. Insist, if necessary, that they do at least one sport or activity and get involved, by driving them to practice, buying the kit and so on.

Keep Talking

This one is probably the most important and it comes up over and over again. Keep the communication channels open. Keen calm, even if your teenager is yelling, and let them know you're around and listening. They will need you as they navigate the choppy waters of pre-adulthood.

Deal with Conflict

Not easy, but necessary. Rows just don't help so aim not to engage in shouting matches and to keep the number of rules and boundaries few and simple. And be prepared to let the less important things go. If they want to live on cereal for a week at a time, well, OK, because eventually they will get bored.

Balance Rules and Negotiation

This follows from conflict minimizing. Have a rule if it's about safety and wellbeing, otherwise be prepared to talk things over and compromise. A teenager with some freedom is far less likely to stray into dangerous territories like staying out late, not telling you where they are and drinking too much alcohol.

Focusing on Solutions

Teenagers have many qualities and attributes that are highly desirable, attractive and useful. A world without new thinking, boundary-pushing, passion and energy would be dull and unlikely to grow and develop. As a parent, you can choose to view your teenager in this way and to be solution-focused. Solution-focused brief therapy is an approach that is based upon the following core principles:

- People have what it takes to deal with problems.
- Every problem has a solution.
- The possible solutions are infinite.
- The problem is the problem, not the person.

- If an approach works, do more of it.
- Illuminate and focus on what works.
- If an approach does not work, do something different.
- Focus on future possibilities and solutions.
- Choose to be part of the solution or you will remain part of the problem.
- Unique problems require unique solutions.

Here is a brief summary of a solution-focused brief therapy plan of action:

- Imagine how life would be without the particular problem you are dealing with – what would be happening that isn't happening now and vice versa?
- Acknowledge the problem – BRIEFLY.
- What strengths and resources can you draw upon?
- When has the problem been less evident or even absent and what were people doing/not doing?
- What is your goal? Keep it simple/specific, achievable, observable and realistic.
- Agree a plan of action.

Troubled Teenagers

We hear often enough about the worst aspects of the teenage years but, in the majority of cases, these are transient and relatively short-lived. It's a question of 'keeping the faith', remembering that the values you have lived out all through your child's life have not gone away and will eventually be more evident, in combination with the values that they have worked out for themselves.

Commonplace teenage troubles include:

- Relationship problems
- Anger
- Withdrawal
- Depression
- Aggression
- Issues to do with sexuality and sexual behaviour
- Learning
- Lifestyle choices involving alcohol and drugs

As has been stressed throughout this book, if problems such as the ones above are so severe that they are affecting your child's everyday functioning, health and wellbeing, seek professional help. Your own personal and social resources may be insufficient for supporting your teenage child and the objectivity, clinical skills and knowledge of professionals, such as an educational psychologist, GP or local Child and Adolescent Mental Health Service (CAMHS), frequently make a big difference to the situation. School staff such as year heads, teachers with responsibility for pastoral care and the Special Educational Neds and Disability Coordinator (SENDCo) may also be able to help in giving you information about available professional help. Organizations like the National Children's Bureau and Childline can also be a mine of information.

Helping Your Teenager to Keep Safe

Everyone needs good 'keeping safe' skills, and teenagers particularly so. The key terms to bear in mind are risk assessment and risk management. This means being realistically aware of threats to personal health and wellbeing, and then deciding whether or not to engage in an activity or to be in a particular situation or choose particular people with whom to interact. It also means trying to reduce or eliminate these risks.

Helping to keep your teenager safe means talking to them about all these risks and difficulties they might encounter, and about how they would handle these. Often teenagers just haven't thought about what might happen; they plunge into an invitation or new situation and then find they can't get home or don't like the people they're with, or have drunk too much. Talk to them about exit strategies – having emergency funds for a taxi, emergency phone numbers, and always staying with at least one good, trustworthy friend.

K-E-E-P-I-N-G S-A-F-E

This is a helpful mnemonic to remind your teenager of the key things to help them stay safe:

Keeping aware of danger

Eliminating people, situations and behaviours that you know endanger you

Ensure that you have your phone when you're out

Planning and preparing journeys and ideally doing these with friends

Informing trusted others of your whereabouts
Never accept lifts from complete strangers
Getting to know others before being alone with them
Say no when your gut tells you to
Avoiding alcohol and drugs so that you are not vulnerable
Familiar areas and routes are safer than unfamiliar
Every situation is different; stay alert to any risks

CHAPTER 13

Relationships

My little girls are going to grow up and want to have boyfriends, or girlfriends, one day. They are going to fall in love, move in with someone, maybe marry and have families of their own. But first they're probably going to make a whole lot of mistakes and kiss a few frogs. So how can I help them get choosy about the people they date, and judge wisely before they get too deeply involved? And how will I handle it if I don't like the partners they choose?

The teenage years, that often unpredictable, by turns exciting and alarming time, is also when children, fast growing into young adults, become interested in sex and relationships. Talking about sex is a big challenge for many parents, especially if their teenage son or daughter is confused about their sexuality or even their identity. How do we tackle this delicate subject with thoughtfulness and consideration and still give them the information they need?

Weeping teenagers rejected by their first love, convinced they will never find another, are hard to comfort, but rejection is part of life, so we need to know how to help them through it. And, at the same time, we need to get the right messages across about not rushing in too fast, avoiding unwanted pregnancies and attitudes to pornography. We want our children to have a healthy sexuality and to feel good about their bodies. Not always easy with the pressures they face from the media and social media. But we owe it to them to be on hand, willing to listen, give them information and, when need be, mop up the tears. If the foundations of safety, security, good communication, acceptance, empathy and compatibility are in place, a child is likely to develop adult relationships in a healthy and safe manner.

We also need to help them stay safe – to warn them about stalking, about grooming and about predatory people. I need to teach my girls the warning signs – how much attention is too much, when do endless texts from a new person become creepy? They need to be alert, aware and forewarned, without being too scared to have fun.

And then there are the other relationships in their lives – the friends, work colleagues, bosses and family members they will need to get on with throughout their lives. Relationships are a lifelong learning project in which all our past experience contributes to our development and wellbeing. And research shows that having positive relationships with other people is essential for our wellbeing and is the most important predictor of health, happiness and long life. The ability to get on with others and to show compassion and concern to those around you is also one of the most important factors in success, regardless of skills or education.

What Is a Good Relationship?

The answer to this question will vary from person to person but the main themes are probably universal – for adults and children alike, as psychologist Kairen Cullen confirms, based on her clinical practice. The following mnemonic comes out of an exercise that she has done many times with school-aged children, running social and emotional wellbeing groups:

R-E-L-A-T-I-O-N-S-H-I-P

Respect for the whole and unique person, both yourself and the other person

Empathy so that you try constantly to put yourself in the shoes of the other person

Listening

Aiming to give as well as receive support of different kinds, both practical and emotional

Talking about your joys as well as your worries and troubles

Initiating contact as well as being contacted

Only relationships that are honest and based upon mutual respect

Not devaluing relationships with disloyalty or holding on to them for the sake of being able to say you have this relationship

Sharing feelings

Honesty and sharing differences

Investing emotion, energy and time

Positive regard, especially when working through differences

My Relationship Story

I had a great example in my parents' relationship. They shared and cooperated in everything they did, and they both loved family life and one another.

They came from very different backgrounds, so it was amazing, really, that they got on so well. My father's family were not well off at all; he used to talk about sharing baths in the street with the neighbours. There was one bath and they all filled it up and took turns. He was outgoing, funny and cheeky, and my mum, who'd had a much more formal upbringing with very distant parents, fell for him. Mum had not had a close family life – she once told me her father had to check how old she was on her birthday – and she didn't spend a lot of time with her parents. So Dad, whose family were closer and more easygoing, must have seemed like a breath of fresh air.

Of course, Mum's parents didn't approve. Dad was a barber, he started work at fifteen and he loved his job, chatting to customers and being part of the community. Mum's parents had probably imagined someone with a more academic career in finance or the law. But Mum and Dad were determined and they went ahead and married in their early twenties.

Dad's mum died of a heart attack when Dad was twenty-three. It was out of the blue and a terrible shock to him. His sister-in-law, just twenty-nine, died the same week of cancer. So Dad was arranging two funerals and comforting his brother, who was left to bring up a little boy of two. I think those losses showed him that he could deal with almost anything, and made him strong.

Mum is strong too. She grew up in a house where you were never allowed to be ill; her father would glare at her if she coughed, so she would go and cough into her pillow. It's made her very stoical about life's difficulties. Both she and Dad are copers and that helped them when I was attacked.

They always supported one another, stood by one another and cared for and protected one another, and that's what I hope Richie and I will do too.

Before the attack that changed my life, I tended to take all my relationships for granted. There was my mum, dad, brother and sister, my friends from schooldays and the new friends I made when I moved to London to share a flat. Then there were the people I met through my work as an aspiring model and TV presenter, some of them warm and encouraging, others less so – it's a competitive world in fashion and TV, and there are plenty of people willing to trample over you to the top. But I always made friends as I went along. I had a big social life, going out with friends, partying and clubbing. And, of course, there were dates and a few boyfriends, none very serious because I was in no rush to settle down. Life was full and good and I thought it always would be – until suddenly it all changed.

As I recovered from the attack at home with my parents, my world had narrowed down to a very few people. I was in recovery for a long time and inevitably most people I knew moved on with their lives, while I felt mine had stopped. Once again, just like when I was a small girl, my world was my family.

A few very close friends stayed in contact throughout, and I really discovered through them the value of enduring friendship.

241

When I was ready to make contact again, they were there, offering love and support.

Meeting new people became hard for me. I was aware of looking different and of the questions and judgements I got everywhere I went. I preferred to keep my social contact to a small, trusted group. But I also discovered new relationships, with people I would never have met if my path hadn't changed course in the way it did. Medical staff, people who came to work in my charity, or to support it, and the lovely people I work with on my TV shows and books. All of them warm and supportive.

What I wanted, though, was a partner in life. An intimate relationship with a man I could love and trust. And for a long time that seemed impossible. I went on a couple of dates and the guys ran a mile – one actually left me sitting in a restaurant. That hurt and, although I moved on, I did wonder whether I would spend my life alone.

Then a friend persuaded me to go on one more date – and I met Richie. He was – no surprise – very like my dad. Kind, funny, chatty and charming. From the start, Richie saw me, not what had happened to me, but who I was. And we enjoyed one another's company. We laughed together, we understood one another and we very soon began to care deeply about one another.

I feel lucky to have met Richie and I know he feels the same. We fit together in a way that means we both learn and grow, and that's what I think makes a good relationship. We sort out our arguments – neither of us likes shouting – and we listen if there's a problem. And, not least, we trust one another.

I hope we'll be able to pass on to our daughters the ingredients of a good relationship, in the same way that they were passed on to me by my parents and to Richie by his.

EXERCISE:
WHAT CAN PARENTS
TEACH THEIR CHILDREN
ABOUT RELATIONSHIPS?

Take a few minutes to list what is important to you in a relationship. For instance, your list might include honesty, trust, respect, mutual support, humour or reliability. You might also include things that seem less important but still matter, like not smoking, being able to handle money, being self-supporting, keeping fit and healthy.

Now think about your best relationships – partner, friends, family and work colleagues – and what it is that makes them good. Chances are that there will be a good few things off your list, but there might be a few qualities there that you hadn't listed. For instance, I have a friend I see fairly often and we always find we can talk about absolutely anything. Time flies when I'm with her.

Think too about your more challenging relationships and what you would like to change about them. Not just what you'd change in the other person but what you might change between you. For instance, if you have a work colleague who is often critical, you might wish for a relationship that is mutually more appreciative and generous.

Talking to Your Child About Relationships

The things you have listed in the exercise are not necessarily right for others, even your own children, but by doing this exercise you are in a better position to talk to your children about relationships. You will be more able to answer their questions and also to help them when they have difficult experiences and are unhappy about their own developing relationships. You have a wealth of life experience to draw upon and you may choose to share some of this when talking to your child about relationships, although only do this in a way that is appropriate for your child's age, understanding and particular issues. And always acknowledge the fact that the world you grew up in is different from your child's and that they are unique in their own right rather than duplications of you.

Here are some of the key things about good relationships that you might want to tell your child:

Explain the distinction between real-life relationships and those interactions that happen online, which many people refer to as relationships but which are simply contact. Occasionally an online friendship can turn into something more, for instance with someone with similar interests, a bit like what used to be known as a pen-friend in the days when people still wrote letters to one another. But even then, the relationship won't really develop three dimensions until you meet in the flesh.

A good relationship is equal. Both people put into it – if you feel that one is giving more to it than the other, it tends not to last.

In good relationships, people get to know one another. That

means talking, spending time together and letting it grow – whether it's a friendship or a romance. Sometimes rushing in means you end up rushing out again.

In good relationships, people care about one another and treat one another with respect and kindness. They want to make one another happy and to be considerate.

Sharing is important. Sharing information, good or bad, sharing feelings, happy or sad, and sharing the workload, the worries and the lovely moments too.

In a good relationship, you feel good about yourself. If someone tells you they care about you but you feel miserable, then something is wrong.

Ending Relationships

We always hope that happy relationships will endure for ever, but in fact very few relationships do last a lifetime. People move away, lives change, romances end. So it's worth telling your child that sometimes even good relationships come to an end. Most of us look back on a childhood friend we loved, or an early romance that fizzled out. For children especially, friendships can come and go, for all sorts of reasons, like moving schools or changing interests. That's normal, and so is feeling both sad and happy about it when you look back.

It's also alright to end a relationship that doesn't feel right. For example, if:

You feel pushed around, or bullied.

The other person ignores your wishes, or doesn't listen to you.

245

You are asked to do things that make you feel uncomfortable.

You don't look forward to seeing the other person.

You find you are always the boss in the relationship and you don't like it.

You don't have things you like to do together.

Intimate Relationships

It's largely accepted that if you are physically and sexually intimate within a relationship the stakes are going to be higher. In other words, there is a greater risk of being hurt, and a lot of trust and openness is required.

The large majority of (although not all) young people engage in a number of intimate relationships before finding 'the one' for them. The drive to do this is fuelled by their own search for identity, belonging and security, but, inevitably, often ends up in disappointment and sadness. The fortunate ones will have a secure enough family base and positive enough self-regard to cope with this temporary destabilization and will move on, hopefully that bit more wise and more selective.

The best support a parent can give to their heartbroken child after an intimate relationship breaks down is to be there for them to listen, reassure and talk, *at your child's request*. Resist saying 'I told you so', and keep it to yourself if you feel secretly relieved because you couldn't stand their boyfriend/girlfriend. Focus on doing what you can to rebuild their confidence and self-esteem and have faith that their unhappiness will pass. I have mentioned in previous chapters, on trauma and anxiety, what to look out for if you think they are so deeply unhappy that it is affecting their day-to-day life and general health and wellbeing to the extent that they may need professional help, such as counselling.

The danger with a lot of young boys and girls is that they rush in too fast. Girls in particular may like a boy and feel convinced he's 'the one', sleep with him and then feel horrible because he doesn't want to know. And it's a hundred times worse if he's telling all his friends. Of course, not all boys would do this, many boys get hurt too. It's important to tell your child to go slowly in a new relationship, get to know the boy/girl before getting intimate and make sure you can trust them not to show off about the relationship. That kind of judgement often takes time and practice.

Sexuality

As parents, we want our children to have a happy, healthy attitude to sex. We want them to learn about it – but not too fast – and to feel good about their own bodies and have happy love lives with partners who care about them. We hope that they won't be too disappointed and hurt, although we know a little of this is inevitable, and most of all we hope that they won't be abused or exploited. Yet, despite all these hopes, many parents avoid talking to their children about sex and sexuality. Some never do. Some do a little bit, awkwardly, as in, 'Er, do you know what happens? well, it's like this . . .'

The trouble is, if we don't talk to them about this hugely important subject, where are they going to get information from? Other children (mostly inaccurate), school (covers the basics but a lot of vital areas, like love and trust are left out) and the internet (one-dimensional and sadly host to a vast amount of pornography).

We have to do the job ourselves. And we have to be calm, clear, truthful and accurate. If we are embarrassed and awkward, that's how we're going to make our children feel. We need to be straightforward about it. And there's a lot to cover:

The basic birds and bees stuff – and the fact that it's a good thing

Love and closeness and connection and how that makes sex special

Caring for and knowing and respecting your own body, which includes sexual health

Self-respect and not being sexual with someone you don't care for and trust

Pornography, what it is and why it is so damaging

Sexual abuse, its many forms, and what to do to avoid it and, if it happens, to deal with it

Online grooming

Being gay

Gender identity

Our children want information and guidance. They need us to show them the way, set appropriate boundaries and explain to them the dangers, and the joys, of being a sexual adult.

Keep It Simple

When it comes to the facts of sex and reproduction, the best guidance is to answer children's questions. If they don't ask a follow-up question, then they probably have enough information for the moment. If they do, then answer it. Make sure, especially with very young children, not to go off into a diatribe of complex explanations and twists and turns. Just keep it simple. Be truthful and use the correct names for body parts.

That applies to older children and teenagers too. Give them the answers they ask for, truthfully and simply. If you don't know, then say so, you can always say you'll find out and come back to them, or look up the answer together.

Older children and teenagers may want to have discussions with you about the information you give them, and that's fine, but let them lead – don't insist on a discussion if they aren't ready. They may need time to simply digest the information you give them.

Make sure that children of all ages know they can come to you for answers and information and to put right any puzzles or misinformation they have been given.

Loving Yourself

A healthy sexuality starts with caring for and loving your body and yourself. Your child needs to know that her body is precious and lovely, and that no-one has the right to touch it without her permission and she always has the right to say no to any kind of contact. This includes a hug from mum or dad if she's not in the mood. If you respect it when she says no, it will teach her a valuable lesson.

We need girls to see themselves as more than just their appearance. So much of the media focuses on appearance. To counterbalance this, you can help girls to create a positive relationship with their bodies through sports. Experiencing their own strength, stamina and agility can be incredibly good for girls as well as boys.

Gender Identity

This is the hot topic at the moment. Girls will see from media stars like Caitlyn Jenner, the father of the Jenner girls from *Keeping Up with the Kardashians*, who chose to change sex, as well as from all the media coverage of the issue, that it's quite possible to feel you have been born in the 'wrong' body.

Gender is more fluid than ever today, and the way to approach this is to explain what we all have masculine and feminine aspects within us – there's a spectrum of masculinity and femininity in the world and within us too.

It's also important to explain human characteristics and emotions in terms that are not solely male or female. We all have feelings in common; it's never true, for instance, that men are 'hard-headed' and women 'emotional'. Both can be both. You can talk about yourself and the parts of you that feel more male or more female. An open-minded attitude and discussion about this will allow your daughter to be confident in her own gender identity.

Pornography

Your child will almost certainly see pornography. Another child with a phone in school, a computer somewhere or stumbling across it when Googling a word they have heard. Tackle the subject reasonably early, around the time when they might well have been exposed to it – and the average age for this is nine. Where porn used to mean an old copy of *Playboy* under the bed, now it is graphic and unrelenting. Children don't have to look for it, it's right there.

It's important to explain that pornography has nothing to do with loving sex. It is not real, it's fantasy – sex without feelings, which makes boys think they have to be like machines and girls think they have to be ready all the time. Pornography is not real, human sex, it's totally unrealistic and often violent. Talk to your child about it before they see it, because you can't stop them seeing it.

Don't make your child feel ashamed for watching porn. Let them know that being curious about sex is normal and natural, but that intimate, connected adult sex is far more real and rewarding than porn.

Sexual Abuse
The best way to protect your child from sexual abuse is to teach her how to say no, loud and clear. Abuse often happens when a child is afraid, or feels they must comply.

Make sure your child knows that some body parts are private and that people outside your home should only see them with their clothes on. No-one should touch or see or photograph their private parts and they should not be asked to touch someone else's.

Tell them that, if someone makes them feel uncomfortable, they should go and find Mum or Dad or another adult. And no-one should ever ask them to keep a secret, or not to tell Mum or Dad anything.

A Happy Sexuality

We want our daughters – and sons – to feel that sex is a wonderful, intimate, special experience. For it to be like this for them, they will need to:

Go slowly – delay having sex until they are fully grown up.

Be picky about their partners. Wait until they meet someone they love.

Don't do it when drunk (and certainly not on drugs).

Wait until they feel sure. If they have to think about it, they're not ready.

Adeline and Dasia's Story

Fifteen-year-old Dasia was walking around with a big smile on her face and being especially helpful around the house. She even got her homework in on time. 'Something's making you very happy,' her mum Adeline said, curiously, and Dasia blushed. 'I've fallen for someone and he's gorgeous, Mum,' she said. 'Look, he's the coolest guy in the class and he asked me out.' The picture Dasia showed her mum was of a good-looking boy who, in Adeline's opinion, also looked rather conceited.

'Did you say yes?' she asked Dasia. 'You know you can't go out on a school night. And on other nights I need to know where you are and your curfew is 10pm.'

'I know, I know,' Dasia said. 'Don't worry, we're only going for a coffee on Saturday morning.'

Adeline agreed that this was alright, although she felt uneasy about Mark, the boy Dasia had shown her a picture of. She decided to talk to Dasia about taking things slowly, getting to know him and making sure that she could trust him. But Dasia laughed. 'I do know him, Mum, we're in the same class. All the girls are jealous.'

'Has he had any other girlfriends in the school?' Adeline asked.

'Well, yes, one I think, but it didn't work out, she was all wrong for him.'

'It might be worth finding out what went wrong,' Adeline said. 'Ask her, because it will help you to decide if he is a good person.'

Dasia was cross. 'You're making way too much fuss, Mum, of course he's good, he's in a band and he's captain of the football team.'

'Those things are great,' Adeline said. 'But they don't tell you whether he will be kind and thoughtful towards you.'

Dasia flounced off, annoyed that her Mum was doubting Mark. As far as she was concerned, he was perfect. And he'd chosen her!

That Saturday, Dasia went to meet Mark for coffee. She came back two hours later looking strangely subdued, but she told Adeline that the date had been great.

Two days later, Dasia came in from school and burst into tears.

'What's wrong?' Adeline asked, giving Dasia a hug.

'Oh, Mum, I don't think Mark is a nice boy at all,' Dasia sobbed. 'On Saturday he asked me to a party that night. I told him I could only stay out until 10pm and he laughed at me and said I should ignore that and that there would be lots of alcohol and weed at the party. I said no, and he just walked off. Then today I spoke to Emma, the girl he had dated. She told me that he had persuaded her to let him take a topless photo of her. She was in love and thought he was too. But he just dumped her and showed the photo to all his mates. She was humiliated, but she never told her parents because she was so scared of getting into trouble.'

Adeline gave Dasia a tissue and a cup of tea and then said, 'Dasia, I'm so proud of you for saying no on Saturday. It can't have been easy for you to turn down a date with Mark, but you knew that what he was suggesting was wrong.

'I'm also very sorry to hear about what happened to Emma, and I'm very concerned. What Mark did was actually illegal. Emma is under sixteen and Mark and all the boys who looked at the photos could be in serious trouble. Do you think you could persuade Emma to tell the Head of School what happened? Because if he isn't stopped, Mark will do this again, to other girls.'

Dasia was shocked to realize that what Mark had done was against the law. 'I don't know, Mum, I'll talk to Emma,' she said.

A week later, Dasia told her mother that she and Emma had become good friends. They had gone to see the Head together, Mark's parents had been called and he had been suspended.

'You did the right thing,' Adeline said. 'And now I know that you know how to say no when something doesn't feel right, as well as how to stand by someone who has been badly treated. I know it must have been disappointing to find out that Mark wasn't a nice boy after all, but I'm glad you found out before he could hurt you.'

CHAPTER 14

Letting Go

It seems a long way off at the moment, but one day Belle and Penelope will be off – to jobs, their own homes, their exciting adult lives. And I will be sitting in my empty nest eating ice cream and missing them so much it hurts.

Every parent has to let go, because the reality is that we bring our kids up to be able to leave us and go out into the world. If they can do it with confidence and resilience, then we've done a good job. But that doesn't mean it's easy for us. Letting go, waving them off with a big smile and trusting that you've taught them what they need to know and that they can manage their own lives is, as so many parents have told me, incredibly hard. You miss them more than you ever thought you could – their company, their laughter, their energy, their big hugs and their endless curiosity about life. You even miss their loud music, dirty washing and grumpy morning moods. When they go, it leaves a great big hole in your home and in your heart. What do you do? How do you make that transition from being a full-time parent to a new life without them at the centre of it without feeling redundant and lost? How do you manage without feeling needed, without someone shouting, 'Muuuum, where is my football kit/school bag/mobile?'

I haven't reached this point yet, my girls are still small, but already I wonder how I will handle it and I know it's going to be hard. The connection I feel to Belle and Penelope is so deep, it will last for the whole of our lives. But I know that the intensity of caring for a small child needs to give way to stepping back as they grow older, and finally to letting go when they are ready to fly.

My own mum had to let go twice – once when I left home, and again after the attack. It can't have been easy for her either time – the first when I was a headstrong nineteen-year-old determined to have my own life, and the second time, seven years later, after she and Dad had been nursing me at home for two years.

Both times they handled it sensitively, trusting me to manage, and I hope that, when the time comes, I can handle it as well as they did. Because when your child leaves it's another opportunity to model a healthy way of dealing with a new phase. If your grown child sees you deal with your grief and find solutions in your own life, then they will know how to do it too, when their time comes. And if you are positive, appreciating your new freedom, having a little more money available, perhaps finding new interests, then your child will be able to enjoy their own new freedom without needing to worry about you or to feel guilty.

Remember, too, that you are not losing them completely, you are moving to a new phase of this lifelong relationship. They will be in touch, come home to visit, perhaps join you for holidays. There's lots to look forward to.

Diane says:

When Katie was nineteen, she announced that she was leaving home and it took us by complete surprise. Her older brother was at university but Katie didn't want to go – she was at college training to be a beautician and we had assumed she would stay at home at least until she finished her training. But she told us that she was moving in with a friend in Basingstoke, where her college was.

We didn't want her to do it. We thought she was far too young and wouldn't be able to afford it. And to be honest, it was hard for us to understand why she would leave her warm, comfortable home to go and live in a chilly, unappealing flat. But Katie was determined, she'd already done all her planning, knowing that we'd object if she told us, and she said she was leaving the following week.

We sat her down and went through all the figures, pointing out that she was going to run short of money. She wasn't worried, she kept saying, 'It's all fine, I won't use much petrol, I can eat cheaply.'

We realized that she was going, no matter what we said, so we took the decision to help her and be supportive. We wanted to keep the connection, to stay involved. We had bought things for her brother when he went to university, so we did the same for Katie and paid the deposit on the flat. She was so excited, she'd been watching Friends *and she thought it would be like that, but as soon as she got into the flat she realized that there was no tumble dryer, no kitchen equipment and so on, so we helped with all that.*

When Paul left, it was very hard. I used to pass his room and just stand in the doorway and feel the pain of his absence. But at least I knew that he was at university and it was all planned – I'd had time to prepare. With Katie, it was a whirlwind – I was still stunned by the speed of it when she had gone. Suddenly, it was just us and Suzy, who was at school. It helped to have a child still at home, but we worried a lot over Katie and whether she would manage, and I missed her so much. She was such a handful as a teenager, but she had so much energy and she always made us laugh, she was a born entertainer.

She stayed in touch regularly and we helped her out with money when she fell short. Then, after a few months, her friend ran out of money and moved back home. We thought Katie might too, but she would never admit defeat – the quality which later got her through her terrible ordeal – and she moved into a room on her own. It was horrible, to be honest, I could have wept when I saw it, and we didn't like her landlord, but we went ahead and helped her move. We didn't feel there was any choice, it was that or abandon her, and we could never have done that.

I always worried about Katie, the other two had their feet on the ground but she was so adventurous and she trusted everyone. I didn't want to contain her, only to keep her safe. But we knew we had to let her go. You have to let your children make their own mistakes and they learn from them.

We used to go round and see her with food parcels, or some petrol money and she always came home to visit. By the time she had decided to move to London, after a couple of years, we had accepted that she wasn't coming home again.

Katie loved her life in London, but she was quite distant from us during that time. She was living with flatmates and working in a field we didn't know anything about. She would ring and say everything was fine, but we didn't get a lot of detail. I still missed her – I always did, but I was glad she was happy and I looked forward to the times when she would come home, full of chat and longing for a Sunday roast.

Then the attack happened, and everything changed.

It was as though we had to see her through from babyhood to adulthood again, but much faster. When she came home from hospital she was a baby, then within weeks a toddler, and at six months a stroppy teenager. I remember when she wanted to go to the shops on her own and I thought, 'You can't go alone,' but I had to let her. I stood at the end of the drive watching her go and then went inside and paced around, waiting for her to get back. When she came back, I asked if she was alright, and of course she was. At that point, she was wearing a full plastic mask over a bright red face with her hair shaved at the front and, unbelievably, someone had stopped her to ask for directions. She had run away – it just felt too much to try to talk to them. But she coped, as she always does, and I was proud of her.

I remember feelings of hopelessness at one point because I couldn't see what she was going to do in the future and nor could she. It is awful when you can't help your child because you want to fix it when things go wrong. I couldn't find a solution when she asked, 'How can I earn money? How am I going to find a job?' I thought she could stay at home and get a job locally. But even in her injured state, she still wouldn't – once again she sprang it on us, announcing that she'd found a flat in London and was off.

She'd been going to London to stay with friends in Chiswick, who let her use their spare room. She had started her charity by then, just doing it from home. I wasn't prepared for her to leave and I had to remind myself that it was totally impractical in the long run that Katie come back to live with us. We had to go with her choice and not put obstacles in her way.

Of course, we were very worried when she actually moved out. This time she wasn't the bouncy, confident teenager. The man who hurt her had threatened to get her or her family so she was very scared. It took enormous courage to go back to London and start again. The first thing she did was put a big extra lock on her front door, with bolts and chains. There was a policeman living downstairs and he recognized her and said that if there was ever a problem, he was only downstairs. We were so relieved about that.

The first time Katie left with barely a backward glance. This time it was so different, harder to see because she was frightened. She didn't just disappear, during the first week she spent more nights with us than in the flat. All she had there was a couple of chairs and a cardboard box for a table.

I never wanted to hold her back, I was proud of her, but of course I worried more this second time than the first time. We had seen the worst side of humanity.

I am so grateful for technology. We can message one another and I can check in with Katie regularly. When I first left home to go to teacher training college, there was one phone in the hall of the basement. I couldn't just phone home and ask how to boil an egg or find my national insurance number, I had to manage. It did make me self-sufficient and at the time I didn't think about how my parents felt, and they didn't tell me. But with my own children, staying in regular contact has been so precious. I love our WhatsApp messages and instant photos of how my grandchildren are doing. It has helped a great deal with the whole process of letting go.

My Moving Out Story

What was I thinking! Moving out at nineteen into a tatty room with barely any money when I had a nice, secure home and my meals on the table. And yet, I don't doubt I would do it all over again. I was young and innocent and I couldn't wait to experience the world.

My parents, understandably, wanted safety and continuity for me – while all I wanted was excitement, variety and new experiences. I grew up reading a lot, with Mum being a teacher, things like Enid Blyton's Famous Five and I thought I'd love to be out there sleeping in a forest and having adventures.

I didn't even think of danger, I was so sure I was fine and could look after myself. I had grown up in a small village, nothing had ever gone wrong in my life and I felt safe.

When I first moved out, I was working as a beauty therapist, not earning much and working a twelve- or thirteen-hour day at what is quite a physical job. I could just about make ends meet, although there was probably more help from Mum and Dad than I realized. I was in a spa doing a lot of massages and most women chat while you are giving them their treatment. Most of them were well-off and I was living off the back of their exciting lives.

It wasn't long before I got bored and wanted more in my life – it wasn't enough to clean other women's feet and hear snippets about their lives, I wanted to do something I loved. I had a boyfriend at the time and we moved to London together, but we soon split up and I rented a room and then met other people in the same situation and we moved into a flat together.

I had started to try for modelling jobs while I was a beauty therapist, going to auditions, submitting pictures to agencies and so on. I started to get a few jobs and I did some work as a TV extra. It meant hanging around all day for not much money, but at least it was exciting.

At that stage, I didn't tell my parents a lot. I knew they would be embarrassed or disappointed by my modelling, but that didn't deter me – I still carried on. I look back now and think I was misguided. There is no future or security in modelling, but at the time that didn't matter.

After the attack, my parents were my world for quite a long time. Mum was doing all the hospital visits with me. I was twenty-five years old and I looked to them for every need I had in the world because I couldn't trust anybody else – I was too traumatized. Mum had to be my mother, my friend, partner, boss, companion and adviser.

I had no idea of the way forward, I had hardly any possessions, no house, an empty bank account and I couldn't physically work. Until then, I'd only imagined very old people being unable to work, but suddenly it was me.

I remember talking to the benefits people – I was registered disabled and they said that I could get help. But I didn't want to be on benefits, I was determined to find a way to earn money again.

When I did go to London, I found a flat in a really quiet area and it turned out that both my neighbours were police detectives and they offered help if I needed it. The first night I was in the flat, the power failed and all the lights went off. I was so scared, I rang Dad and he said drive home. But I thought, no, I can't give in and drive home on the first night, so I stayed in the pitch dark and went to bed. In the morning, the power was back on.

I know how hard it must have been for my parents to let me go the first time, and I know it was worse the second time, even though I was twenty-six. They were so good, because they didn't make a fuss or tell me I was doing the wrong thing. They believed in me, even though we were all scared.

I hope that, when the time comes, I will let my girls leave home with as much goodwill and support. I know that if they can go off without worrying about me, then I'll have done a good job. And I hope that when the girls go it will be time for me and Richie to enjoy one another a bit more. At the moment, we're at that stage where the children are the main thing we talk about. I hope we can keep the atmosphere in our home full of love, for the girls and for us, and that later on we'll find new things to do and enjoy together.

Preparing to Let Go

Letting go is really a lifelong process that begins when you realize your child is her own person, with her own thoughts, ideas and hopes and dreams. It happens in so many little moments – the end of breastfeeding, her first morning at nursery, first day at school, first playdate, first sleepover, first trip to the local shop. Each time you cheer her on, while praying that nothing goes wrong and waiting anxiously for her to come home and tell you how exciting it all was.

As she gets into her teens, you have to let go a little more. There will be outings with friends, shopping trips, first dates and parties. Later she may learn to drive or have a holiday with friends.

At all these stages, your child is still under your care, you can prepare her, check in with her, hear all about it afterwards, tell her how well she did and commiserate if anything went wrong. But when your child leaves home, it's different. You won't know what they are doing all the time, or who with, and nor should you. She's leading her own life and it's your job to back off, while letting her know you're still there if she needs you.

Throughout this journey, you will be teaching her how to cope with adulthood and all the challenges it brings.

Here are some of the most valuable things your child will need to know before she sets off alone:

- How to budget, use a credit card and run a bank account
- How to cook a few simple, nutritious dishes
- How to organize her time and get herself up and ready in the morning
- How to do basic household cleaning and keep her own space tidy
- How to do her own laundry
- How to register with a local doctor or get medical help
- How to send a professional email

- How to use birth control
- How to fill in forms and deal with official documents
- How to solve a problem or know how to get help if she can't, whether that's a blocked drain or a broken fuse
- How to put a mistake right

If your child is going to be leaving home in the near future, make sure she knows how to do all these things. It will give her confidence in her own ability to cope, and it will give you the reassurance of knowing that she will at least not be wearing grubby clothes and living off tinned beans.

A surprising number of children aren't taught some or all of these things. Some parents get in the habit of doing everything for their children, so don't be one of them. Stick to the rule that if they can do it for themselves, they should. Get them doing chores in the house while they're still young, they will thank you for it when they leave home (and so will their flatmates). One friend of mine said her daughter spent three months putting her clothes in the student launderette machines without soap. She didn't realize you had to put it in. So don't assume anything! Show them the basics while they're still at home.

Let Then Make Mistakes

One of the biggest concerns parents have when their children leave home is that their child is not ready for independence. But remember, if they feel that they are, then they probably are. And if you've taught them everything on the checklist above, then they should be. But, of course, they will make mistakes. And you may have to exert extreme willpower to stop yourself from sorting them out for them.

Here are some of the things that can, and often do, happen:

They get overdrawn at the bank because they 'didn't realize' they'd spent their wage or student loan.

They lose a job for being cheeky/late/forgetting to go in.

They fall out with the friend they're sharing a flat with.

They get a parking ticket.

They binge-watch a TV show and then realize they haven't done the essay that's due in the morning.

They break up with a boyfriend/girlfriend and wish they hadn't.

This is why you teach them how to put their mistakes right. They need to know how to apologize, pay up, make up or, if none of these is possible, how to take it on the chin and learn from it. So, practise saying, 'I'm so sorry, but I know you'll sort it out.' It's not easy, I know. But now is the time to stop being a managing parent, taking charge, and to begin being a mentoring parent, there to offer consultation and advice should they want to ask for it.

The Pain of Letting Go

So, while your child sets off to discover the world, what about you?

The point where your child leaves home for the first time is hugely significant. And while some parents coast through it and feel just fine, most don't. Empty nest syndrome is a real condition and it can leave some parents, especially mothers, feeling bereft. Motherhood is still considered a woman's principal role in life, whether they work or not, so of course the point at which your child leaves will hit you hard. This can be especially true if it coincides with any other major life event, such as the loss of a parent, illness, the menopause or retirement.

You can find yourself feeling some, or all, of the following:

1. Grief

You may feel it coming on bit by bit, or it may hit you in a surge at an unexpected moment. When a friend says, 'How's your daughter doing?' or you walk into her empty room, or you reach for her favourite snack in the supermarket. As tears well up and you feel your throat constrict with the pain of missing her, don't fight it. Find a quiet space and have a cry. You've been nurturing and loving her all these years, so grieving is right. It will pass; it's a process of adjustment, but at the beginning it can feel raw.

2. Resentment

This might be harder to own up to, but it's still pretty common. It goes along the lines of – I spent all those years slaving to give her everything and now she's waltzed off without a backward glance. Yup, that about sums up parenthood. It's the way it's meant to be, but that doesn't mean it's easy. Don't forget though that the reward for all your years of slaving is your child's independence.

3. Jealousy

Your child gets to have an exciting new life (possibly not so exciting in reality, it will have its share of dull and difficult bits) and here you are, looking at the winding down of your life. It's just not fair. A touch of mother–daughter jealousy is pretty common as we face our own ageing and see our children young and beautiful. But would you really go back to being nineteen? Most of us wouldn't. And are you really looking at winding down? There are endless opportunities at any age, so have your own new adventures.

4. Fear

This is probably the biggest concern of all. You may feel afraid for your child. How will she manage without you? What if something terrible happens and you're not there? What if she panics, or doesn't remember her bank card number, or is lonely? The truth is, all these things and more may happen and she will cope. Take a deep breath and trust her to manage her life. After all, you did.

For most of us, these feelings will pass. But if they don't and you find yourself feeling bleak about the future, crying excessively or feeling that life is no longer worthwhile, then do go and see your GP and ask for help.

L-E-T-T-I-N-G G-O

Here's a lovely mnemonic to help you think about the more positive aspects of letting go:

Learn from the other changes that have happened throughout your life as a mother

Enjoy the new opportunities and challenges that this part of your mothering life brings

Talk to other mothers and carers about the highs and lows of letting go

Tell your child that you are proud and excited about their growing independence

Independence for your child means more independence and choice for you as a mother

Nests become empty when the young leave – consider some changes to your home, whether it means moving or using the living space in a different way

Gather new ideas, new people and new possibilities

Give the emotional/physical/social energy that has been used in your mothering other outlets

Open your door (and heart) to the other important people your child brings home

Taking New Paths

Although it might not feel like it, this is the point when you can make some new and exciting choices about your own life. It's time to think about all those things you wanted to do but put to one side because there wasn't time. Or the friends you haven't seen for ages. Or the course you loved the look of.

Try replacing the phrase 'letting go' with 'taking new paths'. Instead of reminding us of loss (letting go), it makes us think of new possibilities.

Once you know that your child has started their new life and you have good communication set up between you (a weekly Skype or WhatsApp call, for instance), then it's time to think about your new life and to focus on all the positives.

I've come across all kinds of stories of what mothers – and fathers – have done after their children left home. One trained as an occupational therapist, another started hiking and another went back to her early love, painting, and took an art degree. You might want to join a choir, go skydiving or get involved in volunteer work or community events. There are so many possibilities and new friends and causes that need your time and energy, just waiting.

This might also be the time to put time and energy into your relationship. Chances are that the children took centre stage for the last twenty or so years. And, of course, the point where they leave home can also highlight relationship problems. If that's the case, look for solutions – therapy, talking, time together. And if you're still happy together, enjoy it by doing new things together.

If you're a single parent, then this might be the time to meet someone new. It can be especially hard when your child leaves and you've been the only parent, as Kate and Mia's story shows. But don't forget that there are people out there who would love to meet you. So be brave.

Kate and Mia's Story

When her daughter Mia left to go to university Kate knew she would miss her. But she wasn't prepared for the feelings of desolation and grief that overwhelmed her. She told herself that Mia would be back for the holidays, that she had promised to call every week and that she could go and visit Mia. But none of that helped. As Kate sat in Mia's room, looking at the crumpled bedding, she sobbed. It felt as though her life was over. She was about to turn fifty and was pretty sure she was starting the menopause. She felt old, redundant and heartbroken.

Kate and Mia had been especially close since Mia's dad had died when she was five. John had been killed in a car accident, and it was Mia who kept Kate going in those bleak days afterwards. Mother and daughter grew extremely close and always got on well. There had never been any screaming matches or major problems. Mia had been bright and worked hard at school, and they were both excited when she got a place at university to study Biology.

What with being mum to Mia and working full time as a medical receptionist, Kate had never remarried. She'd been asked out once or twice, but felt she didn't want to bring someone new into Mia's life, so she stuck to socializing with a couple of close friends. The trouble was, by the time Mia left for a uni three hours away, Kate's two closest friends had also moved away.

For several weeks, Kate felt really down. The house felt

empty, and although she went to work each day, her life felt empty and pointless. She couldn't imagine what the future held, it felt bleak and empty.

It was a colleague at work, Susie, who noticed how down Kate was. She suggested lunch and over a sandwich asked Kate how she was finding things since Mia went to university. 'I should feel so happy, she's done so well and I'm really proud of her,' Kate admitted. 'But I just feel miserable.'

Susie said she'd felt the same way when her son Joe had left home two years earlier. 'It hit me hard,' she said. 'I had to make a decision to pick up my life again or I would have gone into a depression.'

Susie said she had decided to join a book club and to get a dog. 'I never had time for a dog before, but I adopted a little rescue dog, Milly, and she's been so good for me. I have to get out and walk her whether I feel like it or not. And I've made friends with a couple of other dog walkers. I love my book club too. We chat about the book we're reading, but we also have a glass of wine and some food and natter about life. Why don't you come along next week and try it?'

When Kate hesitated, Susie reminded her that she owed it not just to herself but to Mia to make a go of things. 'You don't want Mia feeling guilty for going and worried about you, do you?' Susie said gently.

Kate was aware that Mia already worried about her, and she promised herself she would change this. She agreed to go to the book club and to her surprise she really enjoyed it. Several of the mums there were going through their children leaving and it felt good to talk about it and to laugh over a glass of wine.

After that, Kate made an effort to fill the hole in her life. She joined a Pilates class and started going on weekend walks with a friend from the book club. When Mia came home for Christmas she was delighted to find her mum relaxed and happy.

A year later, Kate met a new man, Tim, the brother of her book club friend, and after six months they moved in together. 'Honestly, Mum,' Mia joked. 'I've been gone for five minutes and there's no stopping you.' She gave Kate a hug. 'I'm proud of you, Mum, I know it wasn't easy when I left. You refused to be sorry for yourself and that takes guts.'

CHAPTER 15

Adult Daughters

The relationship that adult daughters have with their mothers can be a fraught one at times: intense, loving, fulfilling and frustrating – and sometimes all of these at once. But if you can make the transition successfully to becoming two adults who see each other as people, as well as mother and child, it can be a wonderful, deep and rewarding relationship.

The focus in mother–daughter relationships is often on the transition to adolescence and the familiar tensions that happen then. But the time when the daughter makes a transition to becoming an adult can be even more fraught, because this is the point when a mother has to let go of twenty or so years of mothering and see her child as capable and independent. For some mothers, it's not easy to give up the role they have played for so long and step back. At the same time, the daughter may hesitate about standing on her own two feet and making her own decisions, still looking to her mother for support.

This relationship has such a history that it sets it apart from all others. For nearly two decades, it has been so all-consuming and intense that it has defined both mother and daughter's sense of self. For the mother, her sense of self will rely on whether she feels she has done a good job or not, regardless of whether she worked outside the home. For the daughter, her sense of self as she grew up was dependent on her connection to her mother. Because of this, it is seldom a smooth relationship of equals. There is often tension and a push–pull dance of competitiveness, with both jostling for the upper hand.

Having said that, it can be, and so often is, richly rewarding. In most cases, the relationship brings both happiness and frustration, conflict and joy. It can give us insight and understanding because we are so often mirrors to one another, seeing in each other the things we want to change about ourselves, as well as the things we are proud of and love.

Some mothers and daughters are best friends. Others rarely see one another, perhaps living far apart. Many settle for talking once a week. Some talk about absolutely everything going on in their lives, others either battle all the time or go out of their way to avoid conflict. And for most of us, there's an element of all these things.

In the end, the relationship you have as an adult with your mum is one most of us treasure. Whether you're annoying one another or laughing together over a shared memory, turning to one another for advice or sharing life's most important moments, it's special and those of us lucky enough to have it would not be without it.

The Changing Roles

'When I was a boy of fourteen, my father was so ignorant I could hardly stand to have the old man around. But when I got to be twenty-one, I was astonished at how much he had learned in seven years.'

This brilliant quote from author Mark Twain was written over 150 years ago, and yet it is as true now as it was then – until you are an adult yourself, it is impossible to appreciate what it is that makes a person adult.

Twain sums up the way so many of us look at our parents in a different light once we reach adulthood ourselves. We finally 'get' them, and instead of being continually annoyed by them, as so many of us were when teenage, we see them through fresh eyes.

For mothers and daughters, there's a critical moment when the daughter suddenly realizes that her mother is another woman with her own problems and experiences. Until then, her mother is all-knowing, all-powerful, sometimes infuriating, sometimes wonderful, but not simply a person.

I remember the 'Aha!' moment when Belle was born, when I understood my mother's urge to protect and nurture me, because I felt it myself for my own child. I felt such a strong bond with my mum then, and all I wanted was to say 'sorry' for all the times I was a pain!

Most of us will have experienced a moment like this, a recognition of what our mothers went through and what they have given us. It's all part of the shift as we move into separate lives, linked by our common bonds, family and love.

Research shows that the mother–daughter bond remains strong throughout our lives. And at midlife, around the age of forty, up to ninety per cent of women report good relationships with their mothers.

Can you ever stop being mother and daughter? The answer is, not really. In most cases, mothers continue to mother and daughters still seek their mother's approval throughout their lives. It's hard to change the roles we had all through the first part of our lives together. But at the same time we can learn to separate from those roles enough to see one another through fresh eyes. We can appreciate one another as women, respect our right to make our own decisions and give one another support and friendship.

Key to adapting our roles as mother and daughter is good communication. We need to be able to share our thoughts, to settle our differences and to compromise.

The way we sabotage one another is through criticism. It's the biggest source of complaints about adult mother–daughter relationships. Mothers find it hard to pull back and let their daughters lead their own lives and do things in their own ways. Well-meant 'advice' can come across as critical and daughters bristle. And, of course, it can go both ways, daughters can be critical too.

In today's world, mothers have to accept that their daughters might put a career before marriage and children, that they might delay having children or choose not to have them at all, or that they might have them without marrying, or choose to live in a same-sex relationship. And any of these choices might challenge their mother's expectations and lead to disappointment. This is where mothers have to step back and keep quiet. And daughters have to recognize that, for their mothers, the unfamiliar can be challenging.

Your child may choose a very different life from the one you did, but this shouldn't reduce your own positive self-regard as a mother and your capacity to feel loved, effective, autonomous and competent. Ideally, your relationship with your adult child will be cooperative and dependable, and if it isn't, then it's a question of communication and negotiation. Good communication can be helped by asking your adult child what *they* would like from you. The mother, by definition, has generally been the one who knows most and has the ability to solve problems for the child but when the situation involves two adults then it changes. It's not only fine to admit that you don't have all the answers, it's vital, and the relationship between you and your adult daughter will benefit enormously from this honesty on your part.

In the end, it's all about finding the balance. You long to spend time together, but you need to know when to pull back too. It's great to talk, but listen too. Give advice, but when it's asked for, and even then give it with love and respect. Don't hurt one another needlessly.

If you can share unconditional love and positive regard, tenderness and mutual recognition of life's difficulties and challenges, then you will have a relationship that brings both depth and contentment.

Me and My Mum

I think Mum and I would always have got on well as adults once I passed my wild teenage years, but sharing a major trauma and the recovery years has brought us very close.

It was only later, working with families through my charity, that I realized that many parents go to pieces at a time of crisis. Some fall apart and some never recover mentally from seeing their children go through traumas. That put things into perspective for me, because my parents went through an absolutely awful ordeal – shocking, heartbreaking, terrifying and life-changing – and yet they managed to stay calm and strong, and to hold it together no matter how awful things got.

Mum dealt with seeing me close to death, without a face and in terrible pain. She dealt with the medical side, the legal side, the endless physio and nursing that I needed and my abrupt mood changes and terrors. She did it without complaining and without losing her stability and for that she – along with my dad – will always have my respect and admiration and gratitude. Mum had to be my everything and she did not let me down, she kept her own tears and trauma private, and she was there for me every step of the way. I'm a determined person and, while I'm a lot noisier and more extrovert than Mum is, I think I got that determination from her.

Without the love and care and backing of my parents, I could not have rebuilt my life in the way that I have. They probably don't know how much I owe them, because they're modest people, but they got me through an ordeal that might have ended everything.

I'm proud of the life I have now, and I'm a lot more sensible than I was when I first left home. I value security and I do think about the future. At the same time I still love change and excitement, I love life and I want to see everything that's out there. I'm lucky in having found a career that gives me both sides. I have a job that has freedom of expression and fulfils my adventure itch, but I'm keenly aware of the need to build a secure future too.

There have been many times, over the years, when I've thought, 'You were right, Mum.' Something I rarely, if ever, thought before the age of twenty! But looking back to my childhood, I realize how valuable the safety and stability at home was. My parents never raised their voices or yelled at one another. They were incredibly united and that was probably one of the biggest influences on me – it's how I want to be with Richie; standing together as one.

It still comforts me to know that my childhood home is there, as certain as ever, no matter where I am. Even now, I know that if there was a disaster I could go back and my parents would give me the same shelter and love and support.

Now that I have children of my own, my relationship with Mum has moved into a new phase. Having been through the tragedy, we're enjoying the happy side of life. Mum adores the girls and they're both named after her. Belle's second name is Elizabeth, a name Mum and I share as a second name, and Penelope's second name is Diane.

When Belle was born, Mum had been diagnosed with cancer. Always reluctant to burden us, she hadn't told us for some time, because I was newly pregnant when she got the diagnosis. The day Belle arrived, Mum was in the middle of treatment and I thought she might not be able to come and meet her first grandchild, but then she and Dad appeared in the hospital and I was so happy – it meant the world to me for her to be there.

Her diagnosis shook all of us, but Mum coped with it in her own, calm, dignified way and she has never let it overshadow the joyous side of family life. Now she has three grandchildren – Suzy had a son a few months before Penelope was born – and they bring her enormous pleasure.

Mum would never push her opinions on us, she is incredibly respectful and waits until we ask; and we do, all the time. Mum is my go-to advice centre and I know it's the same for Suzy. I call her at least five times a week.

These days, I have a lot of different roles, in my work life and my family life. And I like to think that Mum can see this and is proud of me. I hope she can enjoy what my life is now and I think we can relate to one another more. When we appeared on *Loose Women* together in spring 2017, it was fun and we went out together afterwards.

Mum taught me always to see my problems in perspective, compared with other problems in the world, and that has stood me in good stead. It stopped me from becoming too self-obsessed and made me realize that you can choose the way you react.

These days I have a better balance in my life, more strategy in the way I move forward and I regularly stop and take stock. I also think, every day, about the things I am grateful for; my recovery, my husband and children, my work. I appreciate the small things; feeling well, having a lovely breakfast, a hug from Richie, a giggle with the girls. And every day I think about Mum and how she has always been there for me, and how grateful I am for that.

Diane says:

You never know what is going to happen in life. Roles and positions change all the time and you have to adapt. Today, Katie is doing things I never dreamed she would do and that I could never have done, and it makes me feel very humble and proud. She fought back against huge odds and she came through and I will always be full of admiration for her courage and spirit.

We've been through a long journey together, and there were moments when we couldn't see half an hour ahead, let alone to the life Katie has made for herself. I am enormously happy for her and so glad that we are enjoying the good things in life now.

My grandchildren are an absolute delight. When Belle was on the way, I was in treatment and I didn't feel well, so I didn't expect to be able to go to the hospital when she was born. It was a three-hour drive and I told Katie's dad the night before that I couldn't do it. I was crying, and I rarely cry.

Then I woke up in the morning and felt absolutely fine and I said to David, 'Let's go.'

When I walked into the room and saw Katie and Richie smiling and Belle, so tiny and perfect, it was a wonderful moment. Holding her was like the first time I held Katie.

Watching Katie with Belle over the last four years has been a joy. And then Penelope came along and that was another wonder. A second gorgeous little girl.

Katie really wanted to be a good mother, wife, homemaker and a career woman too, and I think she found it all very challenging. But she has achieved it where I don't think I could have. She accepted help when necessary, she put her family's needs before her own, and she worked – and still works – extremely hard. I am full of admiration for the way she is leading her life. Everything she does is for the benefit of her family. She wants the best for Belle and Penelope and she is a fantastic role model. I am very impressed by the guidance she gives her girls every day. She talks to them a lot; she explains things when they ask questions and she reads stories and sings songs and dances with them. Their house is always noisy and lively! But I also like the way Katie expects the girls to have good manners – she insists on please and thank you, and 'May I have?' not 'I want.' She tells them off for being rude and expects them to behave in public. This is how we brought up our children, so I am glad to see she is passing on similar values to hers.

One of the many reasons why I admire Katie is how she lives every day with what has happened to her. Every morning when she opens her eyes, every time she looks in the mirror, every time she swallows her food, she is made aware of the effects this attack has had on her. Despite numerous medical procedures, there are things that will never be put right. She has had to learn to live with this reality every day of her life. I cannot imagine the frustration of some of her limitations: not being able to eat whatever you like without the fear of choking; having permanently blurred vision in one eye that can't be fixed with glasses; washing out her nose every single night; the tightness in her neck when she turns her head. She copes with all this without complaining even though it must get her down sometimes. I can identify a little bit with this feeling, as I am 'living with cancer' as the phrase goes. I feel well and look well most of the time but I have this knowledge hanging over me and sometimes it makes me feel uncertain about the future. Katie shows so much strength in the way she deals with her situation. She refuses to let others see the effect it has on her life and I think this attitude helps us both. I admire and am inspired by her resilience and I hope that, perhaps, she feels the same about me.

What Kind of Mother–Daughter Relationship Do You Have?

While every adult mother–daughter relationship is different, it is possible to see a few patterns emerge. It can be quite entertaining looking around at the mother–daughter relationships you know and spotting the roles they play with one another. And while no-one loves you in quite the same infuriating, intense and yet passionately supportive way that your own mother does, you may find the two of you do fit into one of the common themes.

Love–Hate

They'd be lost without each other, but this mother and daughter will always have their fights. There are times when they refuse to speak to each other, when they battle ferociously, when they disagree passionately and when they demand, indignantly, that their families and friends see how absolutely unreasonable the other one is. But at the same time they really do love one another, and they seldom go a day without talking to one another – unless they're refusing to! They probably don't live far from each other either, they're still pretty closely attached. Both are likely to be outspoken individuals. They're critical and quick to inflame, but in the end they both feel the other is the most important person in the world.

Best Friends

This mother and daughter love to talk everything over, to go out together, to swap clothes and to get involved in the details of one another's lives. When others say, 'You look like sisters,' the mother loves it. She likes to feel youthful and cool and expects to know about every aspect of her daughter's life. The trouble with this relationship is that it can become overwhelming. There's a danger that the daughter will feel invaded by her mum. On the other hand, she may love the relationship as much as her mum does. They're like perpetual teenagers together, having never fully let go of one another. There's also a possibility with this relationship that the mum just isn't facing her age and stage of life. In denial, she wants to be 'one of the girls' at her daughter's hen night and just doesn't know when to take a back seat and claim a little wisdom and dignity.

Weekly Caller

Lots of mothers and daughters rely on the weekly call, either because they live far from one another, as is often the case, or because it suits them to keep a connection but keep some space too. This is often the pattern with a daughter who has recently left home and who is busy making her own life and doesn't want her mum too involved in it. She wants the connection, within limits, but she's still trying to shake off those maternal bonds. The trouble is that it is very easy for this kind of contact to become a weekly 'duty call' that leaves both of you feeling unsettled and unsatisfied. Ideally, you call because you genuinely want to hear about what the other is up to and perhaps because there is a need from either one of you for emotional or practical support. Make sure that visits home are warm and special, so that you both know how appreciated you are.

Mum as Rock

In this relationship, the mum is dependable, solid and always there. She will offer practical and emotional support; she may do the childcare, house-sit, sort out problems and turn up in a crisis. This kind of mother sounds lovely, because she is unlikely to be critical and will seldom say no, but because she can't or won't speak up for herself, there's a danger that she will feel taken for granted and become resentful. No-one really wants to be at someone else's beck and call. So it's important that the daughter in this set-up is appreciative and doesn't assume her mum will step in. Asking her if she minds, spoiling her sometimes and thanking her fully all make a huge difference.

Reverse Roles

This is what happens when the daughter takes the mother role. It is far more likely when both are much older – the mother into old age, the daughter middle-aged. But it does also happen with much younger mothers and daughters – think Saffy in *Absolutely Fabulous*. This kind of daughter has always been more responsible than her mother, who thinks of herself as forever young. It often happens when the mother is uncertain of herself, struggling emotionally or under pressure, and the daughter worries about her. It's common with single-parent families, when the child is aware that she only has one parent and all her emotional investment lies there, so she worries and sees herself as responsible for her mother's welfare. It can be a pattern that lasts throughout their lifetimes, if one or other doesn't step out of it.

Well Balanced

In this scenario, mother and daughter are both thoughtful and respectful. Not perfect, because none of us are, but aware of their own shortcomings and willing to learn and to try to change. This mother and daughter try hard to listen to and understand one another. They ask if they can help but don't dive in or assume anything. They don't criticize but they do say truthfully if there's a problem or they feel hurt or disappointed. Conflict is resolved in an adult way. While they love one another deeply, they both know that they are not dependent on one another because once you are an adult while it's lovely to have a mother, you don't need one. Friends and partners, yes, but not parents because their job has been done.

Doing It Differently

No adult daughter wants to be exactly the same as her own mother. Especially when it comes to bringing up her own children. Some do it very differently indeed, while others tweak the formula in their own style.

But even if a daughter's mothering style is the largely the same as her own mother's, the likelihood is that there will be differences of some sort, and these have to be managed and embraced rather than becoming the source of conflict. For mothers, it can be tough to see that your adult daughter doesn't always follow your style or your rules. But the wise mother of an adult daughter who becomes a parent herself will approach the whole situation very similarly to how they managed the teenage years. A solution-focused and collaborative approach is likely to ensure that your relationship stays positive and you can be supportive rather than bossy and intrusive.

So even if you feel put-out to discover that your daughter uses disposable nappies when you always sang the praises of washing real ones (or vice versa) and even if you think your grandchildren have far too much leeway when it comes to manners/bedtime/technology – the golden rule is, don't say so. Your daughter has a right to do things her way, and unless you have a serious concern about health or danger, you need to accept it.

Things not to say:

- Well, I suppose you're doing it your own way.
- We'd never have done that when I was a young mother.
- I'll just keep out of the way, then, since you seem to have it all sorted out.
- Are you sure it's safe?
- For goodness sake, let me do it.

What to say:

- Looks as though you've got it all in hand, well done.
- What can I do to help?
- What a great idea, wish I'd had that when I was a young mum.
- Cup of tea, anyone?
- You're such a good mother.

For daughters, it can help to sweeten the pill if you acknowledge the differences generously. As in, 'Mum, I think it's brilliant that you always washed the nappies, but these days disposable ones can be eco-friendly and I've decided the time saved is worth it for me.'

Or, 'Thanks, Mum, it wouldn't have been the same without you.' After all, who else can you count on to always be on your side?

Exercise: My Wish List

This one is for the mother in the mother–daughter relationship. It can help to give a broader perspective if you're struggling with feeling left out, or with your daughter doing things very differently. Think back to the most challenging part of your own early mothering years and write a wish list for what you would have liked at that time.

What would you like others – your own mother included – to have said and done? What would have helped you most? What did you learn that you hadn't known at the time?

Chances are a little tenderness, thoughtfulness and respect might have made a real difference. And that's what you can give your own daughter now.

Falling Out

No matter how much mother and adult daughter love one another, they will almost certainly fall out at some point. Research shows that tension between mothers and adult daughters – even in essentially loving relationships – is more the norm than not.

There are those who don't fall out, of course, but most do, although they can do it in very different ways. Some just remain tight-lipped, holding all the tensions inside (potentially for a very long time), while others explode into full-on war and everyone around gets pulled into the battle. And there's just about every degree in between too.

The good news is that the relationship between mothers and their adult daughters is one in which both sides handle being upset with one another better than in any other relationship.

No matter how bad the row, both sides have an investment in keeping the relationship and in the family as a whole. They don't want a rift or to lose one another.

The problem is often that a mother finds it hard to acknowledge that her daughter is an adult. She feels that she is not needed any more, her role has changed and it can be hard to face. So she offers 'advice' and criticism, determined to show that she is still the one who knows best. This frustrates the daughter, who feels she is being treated like the child she once was, instead of the woman she now is.

On the other hand, a daughter may overreact to what she hears as criticism because she gives her mother's opinion more weight than it should have. A daughter, adult or not, longs for her mother to see her as perfect, when, unfortunately, her mother is the person most likely to see her flaws. The daughter still has her mother in the 'all-powerful' role she once occupied. In fact, it's usually the daughter who has more power at this stage. She is the one who controls aspects of the relationship such as frequency of meeting and access to grandchildren.

Conflict situations are made worse when one or both parties involved withdraw or avoid talking about their differences. Equally common is the tendency to try to smooth things over and to be over-conciliatory.

As an alternative to both of those approaches, this is a plan that can work if both of you are willing to sit down and talk:

- Clarify exactly what the conflict is about. Is this a grudge or difficulty that has history or is it a relatively new development?
- Try to establish which underlying values are being threatened or compromised.
- What is at stake? What are the imagined wins and losses for both of you?
- Is anyone else involved, such as fathers (senior and/or junior), other relatives from the immediate and extended family or family friends? Might there be someone who can help you to work out a resolution?
- In an ideal situation, what would be the best outcome for both of you?
- What compromises are possible?

Try to remember that the problem is in the interaction or relationship between both of you. The relationship between mother and daughter is a very special and unique one and the hard work involved in having as good a relationship as possible will pay dividends. However, the emotional ups and downs can be particularly intense so the more 'emotional intelligence' you can bring into play the better.

Almost every mother–daughter duo has its own 'hot button' – that one topic on which you can never see eye to eye. Every time the topic surfaces, it gets the juices flowing and you can feel an argument looming. So, put it to rest, if you can, and if you can't, agree not to press the hot button – ever.

Conflict checklist:

Welcome your mother/daughter's insights and opinions without being dismissive.

When you find yourself feeling defensive, take a deep breath and reconsider.

Let go of the idea that either of you knows best.

Express support and confidence in the other's choices.

Try to worry less – most of what we fear doesn't happen.

Do things together, as well as meeting to talk. Activities shared can deepen a relationship.

Let go of jealousy of the other people in her life.

Remember that there are times when it's best to say nothing.

Practise saying 'You're wonderful.' It melts barriers.

Be willing to apologize – and to forgive.

Anita and Julie's Story

Julie had always struggled with her mum Anita's strong opinions and interference in her life. As a teenager, she had fought back and they'd had many shouting matches. But as Julie reached her twenties, there was no sign of Anita backing off. Anita felt she had a right to an opinion on everything – Julie's job, her flat, her boyfriends and her clothes. And most of Anita's opinions were critical. Her flat was a mess, her boyfriend not good enough, her job below her ability level. She loved Julie deeply, they both knew that, but Julie was reaching the point where she knew either her mum had to back off or she would need to break away and stop seeing her.

Julie struggled with her mother's opinions. She felt, deep down, that her mother might be right, and that led to discontent with her life. Why was she getting everything wrong?

It was a friend, Zara, who said, 'You're not, your mum is interfering and critical. Maybe she wishes she had the flat and the job and the boyfriend that you have.'

Julie was twenty-five when she sat her mother down and said that, if she didn't stop criticizing and interfering, Julie would stop seeing her. Anita was outraged, but Julie stayed calm and stuck to her point. 'Stop telling me I'm getting everything wrong, Mum, it just gets me down.'

Anita looked shocked and then burst into tears. 'I'm sorry,' she sobbed. 'I didn't mean you to think that. You're not getting things wrong, you've done so well, better than I ever could.

It's just my habit, I think that if I criticize, you won't get big-headed or take it all for granted.'

Anita promised to change, and Julie hugged her and said, 'I'm going to stop you, Mum, if you start putting down my choices or telling me my flat is a mess. It's my life and I want you in it. But I need to know that you support me and trust me to make my own choices.'

And Finally . . .

I am so glad and grateful that I'm a mum. Despite the broken nights and the conviction that finding five minutes to myself is doomed to be an impossible quest, I wouldn't change a thing. Having my two beautiful daughters has made me feel happier than I imagined possible. With them every day brings something new and surprising – and no two days are ever the same.

Once you have a baby – whatever age you are and whether your baby was planned or medically induced or not – life is never the same again. From that moment on someone else's needs consume you to an extent you would never have believed possible. And most of us experience a feeling of such deep love and protectiveness that it takes our breath away.

Motherhood is wonderful, exciting, overwhelming and humbling. It's also a constant challenge. You wonder if you're getting it right, feel endlessly in demand and, at times, frustrated and tested. There's no giving it back or walking away. It changes you physically (aaargh, nothing fits any more), mentally (I couldn't remember anything beyond my own name for the first few months) and emotionally (I cry at absolutely everything now).

It's an endless learning curve; sometimes it seems the moment you get a grip on one thing there are ten more puzzles waiting to be solved. Motherhood isn't perfect, it's not all rose-tinted glasses, it involves domestic drudgery, loneliness, feeling unappreciated and a level of exhaustion you never thought possible.

They say that on average new mothers go from spending two hours a week caring for someone else to fifty. And at the same time you up your levels of housework by about ten hours a week. And that's before the broken nights. So there's definitely no avoiding the tiredness.

As a mum you learn to live with the unexpected – the tears and meltdowns, the dramas and successes, the grazed knees and the torn shorts, the sudden mood changes (ill and grumpy to well and excited in five minutes) and the smiles and cuddles and crooked little pictures of you with four arms, blue teeth and a crown that can move you to tears.

You also learn to cope with, well, just about anything. You discover skills you never knew you had, you learn to plan, to manage, to give orders and to do three things at once.

There's no instruction manual for motherhood, it's something you learn on the job, and you never stop learning, as my own mum assures me, even when your children are grown. That's why you need a supports system and friends who can laugh with you over the pitfalls and achievements of getting through the day with a child of, well, just about any age.

Bringing up children is a huge task. You hope they will be good, kind, ethical and responsible but, at some point, most days, you fear that you've failed. You want them to be able to contribute to society, and you want them to be happy, healthy and fulfilled in what they choose to do with their lives and in their relationships. All of that is a tall order.

And we so often feel that we get it wrong! What mother doesn't look back on the past week, or month, or year, or twenty years and think, 'well I could have done some things better'. That's why motherhood shreds any ideas you ever had about being a perfectionist. It makes me laugh to think I ever aspired to perfection. As a mother 'good enough' becomes your mantra. And it's the right one, because 'good enough' is enough and getting things wrong comes with the territory.

So if motherhood is looking daunting, or scary, or like a mountain you just might never climb, take heart. The only way to approach it is one step at a time and by reminding yourself that you have depths and resources you have yet to discover. And by remembering that just as the challenges will go on, so will the pleasures. As someone once said, 'There's no way to be a perfect mother and a million ways to be a good one'.

For me, being a daughter and a mother has been illuminating. I am between the generations, my mum before me, my daughters after me. We are all joined by the silver threads of love and inheritance and the connections we find every time we are together. And the real joy lies in knowing that we always will be.

References

Dr Kairen Cullen, *Introducing Child Psychology* (Icon Books, 2011) – a short and helpful guide by the psychologist who advised on *Mothers and Daughters*.

Chapter 1: Becoming a Mum
Donald Winnicott, *Babies and Their Mothers* (Perseus Publishing, 1987).

John Bowlby and Margery Fry, *Childcare and the Growth of Love* (Pelican Books, 1953).

Nancy Julia Chodorow, *The Reproduction of Mothering: Psychoanalysis and the Sociology of Gender* (1978).

Chapter 3: Role Models
Tanya Byron, *Safer Children in a Digital World: The Report of the Byron Review* (2008).

Albert Bandura, *Social Foundations of Thought and Action: A social cognitive theory* (1986).

www.gov.uk

UK Council for Child Internet Safety (UKCCIS) – UKCCIS is a group of more than 200 organizations drawn from across government, industry, law, academia and charity sectors, which work in partnership to help keep children safe online. The Council was established in 2010 following a review by Professor Tanya Byron discussing, and taking action, on topical issues concerning children's use of the internet.

Chapter 5: Body Image

J. Harriger, Age Differences in Body Size Stereotyping in a Sample of Preschool Girls, *Eating Disorders*, 23 (2), 2015.

Chapter 6: Friendships

Guidance on the safe use of social media is now widely available from bodies such as the Department for Education (DfE), Department of Health (DoH), National Society for the Prevention of Cruelty to Children (NSPCC), National Children's Bureau (NCB).

Tanya Byron, *Safer Children in a Digital World: The Report of the Byron Review* (2008).

Professor Tanya Byron's wide-scale review informed the setting up of the UK Council for Child Internet Safety (UKCCIS), a group of more than 200 organizations drawn from across government, industry, law, academia and charity sectors, which work in partnership to help keep children safe online.

Sue Roffey, Tony Tarrant and Karen Majors, *Young Friends: Schools and Friendship* (1994).

Chapter 8: Trauma

Some useful references:

British Association for Counselling and Psychotherapy – www.bacp.co.uk

Cruse Bereavement Care – www.cruse.org.uk – lots of reading material as well as access to direct support and advice

Doris Stickney, *Water Bugs and Dragonflies: Explaining Death to Young Children* (2004) – one of my favourite books for young children on bereavement and grief.

See also all the references given for Chapter 9: Managing Anxiety.

Chapter 9: Managing Anxiety

Some useful references:

Virginia Ironside, *The Huge Bag of Worries* (Hodder, 1996) – a brilliant picture book aimed at younger children but actually good for all ages.

NHS: Anxiety disorders in children – www.nhs.uk/Conditions/anxiety-children/Pages/Introduction.aspx

Young Minds – https://youngminds.org.uk

Royal College of Psychiatry – www.rcpsych.ac.uk/healthadvice/parentsandyouthinfo/parentscarers/worriesandanxieties.aspx

There are also a number of specific organizations online (such as www.anxietycare.org.uk/docs/anxiety.asp and www.anxietyuk.org.uk) but many of these are aimed at adults.

You can also contact the Centre for Child Mental Health

(CCMH), 2–28 Britannia Row, Islington, London N1 8PA, 0207 354 2918, www.childmentalhealthcentre.org

The Director of the CCMH is Dr Margot Sunderland and she has written a series of useful and straightforward books available on the CCMH website: https://www.childmentalhealthcentre.org/ccmh/shop/

These include:
Conversations That Matter
What Every Parent Needs to Know
Bothered
Helping Teenagers with Anger and Low Self-Esteem
Helping Children Locked in Rage or Hate: A Guidebook
Helping Children with Low Self-esteem
Helping Children with Loss
Helping Children Who Are Anxious or Obsessional
Helping Children Who Bottle Up Their Feelings: A Guidebook
Helping Children with Fear: A Guidebook
Helping Children Pursue Their Hopes and Dreams: A Guidebook

Chapter 11: The Guilty Mum

Organizations that might help:

Mumsnet
National Childbirth Trust
National Children's Bureau
Parents' organizations
Care for the Family

Parenting UK

Church/local community groups

Chapter 13: Relationships

FFLAG (Families and Friends of Lesbians and Gays) – www.fflag.
org.uk – a charity supporting the friends and families of gay, les-
bian, bisexual and transgender sons and daughters.